Collins

CW00741466

Collins
Italian
Words

HarperCollins Publishers
Westerhill Road
Bishopbriggs
Glasgow
G64 2QT
Great Britain

First Edition 2009

Reprint 10 9 8 7 6 5 4 3 2 1 0

© HarperCollins Publishers 2009

ISBN 978-0-00-729843-3

Collins® is a registered trademark of
HarperCollins Publishers Limited

www.collinslanguage.com

A catalogue record for this book is available
from the British Library

Typeset by Thomas Callan

Printed in Italy by LEGO Spa, Lavis (Trento)

Acknowledgements
We would like to thank those authors and
publishers who kindly gave permission for
copyright material to be used in the Collins
Word Web. We would also like to thank Times
Newspapers Ltd for providing
valuable data.

PUBLISHING DIRECTOR
Rob Scriven

EDITORIAL DIRECTOR
Catherine Love

MANAGING EDITOR
Gaëlle Amiot-Cadey

PROJECT COORDINATORS
Caroline Smart
Susie Beattie

CONTRIBUTORS
Gabriella Bacchelli
Federico Bonfanti

William Collins' dream of knowledge for all began with the publication of his first book in 1819. A self-educated mill worker, he not only enriched millions of lives, but also founded a flourishing publishing house. Today, staying true to this spirit, Collins books are packed with inspiration, innovation, and practical expertise. They place you at the centre of a world of possibility and give you exactly what you need to explore it.

Language is the key to this exploration, and at the heart of Collins Dictionaries is language as it is really used. New words, phrases, and meanings spring up every day, and all of them are captured and analysed by the Collins Word Web. Constantly updated, and with over 2.5 billion entries, this living language resource is unique to our dictionaries.

Words are tools for life. And a Collins Dictionary makes them work for you.

Collins. Do more.

contents

6 contents

Collins Easy Learning Italian Words is designed for both young and adult learners. Whether you are starting to learn Italian for the first time, revising for school exams or simply want to brush up on your Italian, *Collins Easy Learning Italian Words* offers you the information you require in a clear and accessible format.

This book is divided into 50 topics, arranged in alphabetical order. This thematic approach enables you to learn related words and phrases together, so that you can become confident in using particular vocabulary in context.

Vocabulary within each topic is divided into nouns and useful phrases which are aimed at helping you to express yourself in idiomatic Italian. Vocabulary within each topic is graded to help you prioritize your learning. Essential words include the basic words you will need to be able to communicate effectively, important words help expand your knowledge, and useful words provide additional vocabulary which will enable you to express yourself more fully.

Nouns are grouped by gender: masculine ("il") nouns are given on the left-hand page, and feminine ("la") nouns on the right-hand page, enabling you to memorize words according to their gender. In addition, all feminine forms of adjectives are shown, as are irregular, invariable and gender-changing noun plurals.

At the end of the book you will find a list of supplementary vocabulary, grouped according to part of speech – adjective, verb, noun and so on. This is vocabulary which you will come across in many everyday situations.

Finally, there is an English index which lists all the essential and important nouns given under the topic headings for quick reference.

Collins Easy Learning Italian Words helps you to consolidate your language learning. Together with the other titles in the *Easy Learning* range you can be sure that you have all the help you need when learning Italian at your fingertips.

ABBREVIATIONS

adj	adjective
adv	adverb
conj	conjunction
f	feminine
inv	invariable
m	masculine
m+f	masculine and feminine form
n	noun
pl	plural
pl inv	invariable, with no change to noun in the plural
prep	preposition
qc	qualcosa
qn	qualcuno
sb	somebody
sing	singular
sth	something

The swung dash ~ is used to indicate no change to a word in the plural of a compound noun.

GENDER

In Italian, nouns are either masculine or feminine. Most masculine nouns take the article il. This article becomes l' when the noun begins with a vowel and becomes lo when the noun begins with s+consonant (eg sc, sp, st), or begins gn, pn, ps, x, y or z.
Feminine nouns take la or l' (when the noun begins with a vowel).

Many masculine nouns end in o; many feminine nouns end in a. Both masculine and feminine nouns can end in e.

PLURAL

Unlike English, where you generally add letters (s or es) to make nouns plural, in Italian you change the final letter.
o > **i** (il post**o** > i post**i**)
a > **e** (la pizz**a** > le pizz**e**)
e > **i** (il padr**e**, la madr**e** > i padr**i**, le madr**i**)
Articles change as follows:
masculine: il > i   l' > gli   lo > gli
feminine: la > le   l' > le
Nouns that are imported into Italian (such as bar, computer, menù, sport) stay the same in the plural (*pl inv*). They are generally masculine:
il bar > i bar, il computer > i computer, il menù > i menù, lo sport > gli sport.

PLURAL SPELLING CHANGES

Most nouns ending -co, -ca, -go and -ga often require an h inserting in the plural to retain the hard 'kuh' and 'guh' sounds:
il parco > i parchi, la banca > le banche
il lago > i laghi, la targa > le targhe
Where spelling changes occur in the plural we have included the plural ending.

ESSENTIAL WORDS *(masculine)*

un **aereo**	plane
un **aeroplano**	aeroplane
un **aeroporto**	airport
un **agente di viaggio**	travel agent
l' **arrivo**	arrival
il **bagaglio**	luggage
il **bagaglio a mano**	hand luggage
il **banco**	desk
il **biglietto**	ticket
il **carrello**	trolley
il **check-in**	check in
il **doganiere**	customs officer
l' **imbarco**	boarding
il **noleggio auto**	car hire
il **numero**	number
un **orario**	timetable
il **passaporto**	passport
il **passeggero**	passenger
il **prezzo del biglietto**	fare
il **ritardo**	delay
il **taxi** *(pl inv)*	taxi
il **turista**	tourist; holiday maker
il **viaggiatore**	traveller
il **viaggio**	trip
il **volo**	flight

USEFUL PHRASES

viaggiare in aereo to travel by plane
un biglietto di sola andata a one-way ticket
un biglietto di andata e ritorno a return ticket
prenotare un biglietto aereo to book a plane ticket
fare il check-in del bagaglio to check in luggage
l'aereo è decollato/atterrato the plane has taken off/landed
il tabellone degli arrivi/delle partenze the arrivals/departures board
il volo numero 776 proveniente da Roma/diretto a Roma flight number 776
  from Rome/to Rome

ESSENTIAL WORDS *(feminine)*

un'	**agente di viaggio**	travel agent
la	**borsa**	bag
la	**cancellazione**	cancellation
la	**carta d'identità**	ID card
la	**carta d'imbarco**	boarding card
la	**coincidenza**	connection
la	**dogana**	customs
la	**doganiera**	customs officer
l'	**entrata**	entrance
le	**informazioni**	information desk; information
la	**partenza**	departure
la	**passeggera**	passenger
la	**prenotazione**	reservation
la	**tariffa**	fare
le	**toilette**	toilets
la	**turista**	tourist; holiday maker
l'	**uscita**	exit; gate
l'	**uscita d'emergenza**	emergency exit
l'	**uscita d'imbarco**	departure gate
la	**valigia**	bag; suitcase
la	**viaggiatrice**	traveller

USEFUL PHRASES

ho perso la coincidenza I missed my connection
ritirare la valigia to collect one's luggage
"ritiro bagagli" "baggage reclaim"
passare per la dogana to go through customs
ho qualcosa da dichiarare I have something to declare
non ho niente da dichiarare I have nothing to declare
controllare il bagaglio to search the luggage
voli nazionali/internazionali domestic/international flights

IMPORTANT WORDS (*masculine*)

il	biglietto elettronico	e-ticket
il	corridoio	aisle
un	elicottero	helicopter
il	finestrino	window
un	incidente aereo	plane crash
il	mal d'aria	airsickness
il	pilota	pilot

USEFUL WORDS (*masculine*)

un	assistente di volo	flight attendant
un	atterraggio	landing
i	comandi	controls
il	controllo di sicurezza	security check
il	controllore del traffico aereo	air-traffic controller
il	decollo	take-off
i	diritti di dogana	customs duty
un	equipaggio	crew
l'	imbarco (*pl* -chi)	boarding
il	jumbo (*pl inv*)	jumbo jet
il	metal detector (*pl inv*)	metal detector
il	nastro trasportatore	carousel
un	orario	timetable
il	paracadute (*pl inv*)	parachute
il	posto (a sedere)	seat
il	radar (*pl inv*)	radar
il	reattore	jet engine
lo	scalo	stopover
lo	steward (*pl inv*)	steward
il	terminal (*pl inv*)	terminal
il	vuoto d'aria	air pocket

USEFUL PHRASES

a bordo on board; "vietato fumare" "no smoking"
in ritardo delayed; in orario on time
"allacciare le cinture di sicurezza" "fasten your seat belts"
stiamo volando sopra Londra we are flying over London
ho la nausea I am feeling sick; fare un dirottamento aereo to hijack a plane

IMPORTANT WORDS *(feminine)*

la	cintura di sicurezza	seat belt
la	durata	length; duration
la	mappa	map
la	sala d'imbarco	departure lounge
la	velocità *(pl inv)*	speed

USEFUL WORDS *(feminine)*

un'	ala	wing
l'	altezza	height
l'	altitudine	altitude
un'	assistente di volo	flight attendant
la	barriera del suono	sound barrier
un'	elica *(pl -che)*	propeller
un'	etichetta	label
la	hostess *(pl inv)*	air hostess
la	linea aerea	airline
la	pista (d'atterraggio)	runway
la	rivista	magazine
la	scala mobile	escalator
la	scatola nera	black box
la	torre di controllo	control tower
la	turbolenza	turbulence

USEFUL PHRASES

"i passeggeri del volo AB251 con destinazione Roma sono pregati di procedere all'imbarco all'uscita 51" "flight AB251 to Rome now boarding at gate 51"

abbiamo fatto scalo a New York we stopped over in New York

un atterraggio d'emergenza an emergency landing

un atterraggio di fortuna a crash landing

ESSENTIAL WORDS *(masculine)*

un	agnello	lamb
un	animale	animal
il	bue *(pl* buoi)	ox
il	cane	dog
il	cavallo	horse
il	cinghiale	wild boar
il	coniglio	rabbit
il	criceto	hamster
il	cucciolo	puppy
un	elefante	elephant
il	gattino	kitten
il	gatto	cat
il	giardino zoologico	zoo
il	leone	lion
il	maiale	pig
il	pelo	coat, hair
il	pesce	fish
il	topo	mouse
un	uccello	bird
il	vitello	calf
il	volpe	fox
lo	zoo *(pl inv)*	zoo

USEFUL PHRASES

mi piacciono i gatti, odio i serpenti, preferisco i cani I like cats, I hate snakes, I prefer dogs

in casa abbiamo 12 animali we have 12 pets in our house

non abbiamo animali in casa we have no pets in our house

gli animali selvatici wild animals

gli animali domestici pets

il bestiame livestock

mettere un animale in gabbia to put an animal in a cage

liberare un animale to set an animal free

ESSENTIAL WORDS *(feminine)*

la **cagna**	dog *(female)*
la **gatta**	cat *(female)*
la **mucca** *(pl -che)*	cow
la **pecora**	ewe
la **pelliccia** *(pl -ce)*	fur
la **scimmia**	monkey
la **tartaruga** *(pl -ghe)*	tortoise
la **tigre**	tiger

IMPORTANT WORDS *(feminine)*

la **caccia**	hunting
la **coda**	tail
la **gabbia**	cage
la **zampa**	paw

USEFUL PHRASES

il cane abbaia the dog barks; ringhia it growls
il gatto miagola the cat miaows; fa le fusa it purrs
mi piace l'equitazione *or* andare a cavallo I like horse-riding
a cavallo on horseback
"attenti al cane" "beware of the dog"
"è vietato introdurre cani" "no dogs allowed"
"a cuccia!" *(to dog)* "down!"
i diritti degli animali animal rights
andare a caccia to go hunting

USEFUL WORDS *(masculine)*

un	artiglio	claw *(of lion, tiger)*
un	asino	donkey
il	cammello	camel
il	canguro	kangaroo
il	canile	kennel
il	caprone	billy goat
il	carapace	shell *(of tortoise)*
il	cervo	deer, stag
il	coccodrillo	crocodile
il	corno	horn
il	guinzaglio	dog lead
un	ippopotamo	hippopotamus
il	lupo	wolf
il	maiale	pig
il	marsupio	pouch *(of kangaroo)*
il	mulo	mule
il	muso	muzzle; snout
il	negozio di animali	pet shop
un	orso	bear
un	orso polare	polar bear
il	pipistrello	bat
il	pony *(pl inv)*	pony
il	porcellino d'india	guinea pig
il	puledro	foal
il	ratto	rat
il	riccio	hedgehog
il	rinoceronte	rhinoceros
il	rospo	toad
lo	scoiattolo	squirrel
il	serpente	snake
lo	squalo	shark
il	toro	bull
lo	zoccolo	hoof

USEFUL WORDS *(feminine)*

la	**balena**	whale
la	**biscia** *(pl -sce)*	snake
la	**bocca** *(pl -che)*	mouth
la	**capra**	(nanny) goat
la	**cavalla**	mare
la	**cavia**	guinea pig
la	**cerva**	doe
le	**corna**	antlers; horns
la	**criniera**	mane
la	**foca** *(pl -che)*	seal
la	**giraffa**	giraffe
la	**gobba**	hump *(of camel)*
la	**leonessa**	lioness
la	**lepre**	hare
la	**lucertola**	lizard
la	**mula**	mule
la	**pelle**	hide *(of cow, elephant etc)*
la	**proboscide**	trunk *(of elephant)*
la	**rana**	frog
le	**strisce**	stripes *(of zebra)*
la	**talpa**	mole
la	**tigre**	tigress
la	**trappola**	trap
la	**vipera**	viper; adder
la	**volpe**	fox
la	**zanna**	tusk
la	**zebra**	zebra

ESSENTIAL WORDS *(masculine)*

il **casco** *(pl -chi)*	helmet
il **ciclismo**	cycling
il **ciclista**	cyclist
il **fanale**	lamp
il **freno**	brake

IMPORTANT WORDS *(masculine)*

il **pedale**	pedal
il **sellino**	saddle

USEFUL WORDS *(masculine)*

il **cambio**	derailleur; gears
il **campanello**	bell
il **catarifrangente**	reflector
il **cestino**	pannier
il **Giro d'Italia**	Tour of Italy
il **kit** *(pl inv)* **per riparare le gomme**	puncture repair kit
il **lucchetto**	padlock
il **manubrio**	handlebars
il **mozzo**	hub
il **parafango** *(pl -ghi)*	mudguard
il **portapacchi** *(pl inv)*	carrier
il **raggio**	spoke
il **telaio**	frame
il **tubolare**	tyre

USEFUL PHRASES

andare in bici(cletta) to go by bike, to cycle
sono venuto in bici(cletta) I came by bike
pedalare to pedal
a tutta velocità at full speed
cambiare marcia to change gear
fermarsi to stop
frenare bruscamente to brake suddenly

ESSENTIAL WORDS *(feminine)*

la	**bici** *(pl inv)*	bike
la	**bicicletta**	bicycle
la	**ciclista**	cyclist
la	**city bike** *(pl inv)*	city bike
la	**mountain bike** *(pl inv)*	mountain bike
la	**sella**	saddle

IMPORTANT WORDS *(feminine)*

la	**camera d'aria**	inner tube
la	**discesa**	descent
la	**foratura**	puncture
la	**gomma**	tyre
la	**marcia** *(pl -ce)*	gear
la	**pista ciclabile**	cycle lane
la	**pompa**	pump
la	**ruota**	wheel
la	**salita**	climb
la	**velocità** *(pl inv)*	speed

USEFUL WORDS *(feminine)*

la	**caduta**	fall
la	**canna superiore**	crossbar
la	**catena**	chain
la	**cima**	top *(of hill)*
la	**dinamo** *(pl inv)*	dynamo
la	**luce anteriore**	front light
la	**valvola**	valve

USEFUL PHRASES

fare un giro in bici(cletta) to go for a bike ride
bucare to have a puncture
riparare una gomma to mend a puncture
la ruota anteriore/posteriore the front/back wheel
gonfiare le ruote to blow up the tyres
lucido(a) shiny
fluorescente fluorescent

ESSENTIAL WORDS *(masculine)*

il	cielo	sky
il	gallo	cock
il	pappagallino	budgie
il	pappagallo	parrot
il	tacchino	turkey
un	uccello	bird

USEFUL WORDS *(masculine)*

un	avvoltoio	vulture
il	becco *(pl -chi)*	beak
il	canarino	canary
il	cigno	swan
il	corvo	raven
il	cuculo	cuckoo
il	fagiano	pheasant
il	falcone	falcon
il	gabbiano	seagull
il	gallo cedrone	grouse
il	gufo	owl
il	martin pescatore	kingfisher
il	merlo	blackbird
il	nido	nest
il	passero	sparrow
il	pavone	peacock
il	pettirosso	robin
il	picchio	woodpecker
il	piccione	pigeon
il	pinguino	penguin
lo	scricciolo	wren
lo	storno	starling
lo	struzzo	ostrich
il	tordo	thrush
un	uccello rapace	bird of prey
un	uovo *(pl f uova)*	egg
un	usignolo	nightingale

ESSENTIAL WORDS *(feminine)*

un'	**ala**	wing
un'	**anatra**	duck
la	**gallina**	hen
un'	**oca** *(pl -che)*	goose

USEFUL WORDS *(feminine)*

un'	**allodola**	lark
un'	**aquila**	eagle
la	**cicogna**	stork
la	**cinciarella**	bluetit
la	**colomba**	dove
la	**gabbia**	cage
l'	**Influenza avaria**	bird flu
la	**gazza**	magpie
la	**pernice**	partridge
la	**piuma**	feather
la	**quaglia**	quail
la	**rondine**	swallow
la	**taccola**	jackdaw
le	**uova**	eggs

USEFUL PHRASES

volare **to fly**
volare via **to fly away**
costruire un nido **to build a nest**
fischiare **to whistle**
cantare **to sing**
la gente li mette in gabbia **people put them in cages**
covare un uovo **to sit on an egg**
un uccello migratore **a migratory bird**

ESSENTIAL WORDS (masculine)

il	braccio (pl f braccia)	arm
i	capelli	hair
il	corpo	body
il	cuore	heart
il	dente	tooth
il	dito (pl f dita)	finger
il	ginocchio	knee
il	naso	nose
un	occhio	eye
un	orecchio (pl f orecchie)	ear
il	pelo	hair
il	piede	foot
lo	stomaco	stomach
il	viso	face

IMPORTANT WORDS (masculine)

il	collo	neck
il	mento	chin
il	petto	chest; bust
il	pollice	thumb
il	sangue	blood
il	sopracciglio (pl f sopracciglia)	eyebrow

USEFUL PHRASES
in piedi standing
seduto(a) sitting
disteso(a) lying

ESSENTIAL WORDS *(feminine)*

la	**bocca** *(pl-che)*	mouth
le	**braccia**	arms
le	**dita**	fingers
la	**gamba**	leg
la	**gola**	throat
la	**mano** *(pl mani)*	hand
la	**narice**	nostril
la	**schiena**	back
la	**testa**	head

IMPORTANT WORDS *(feminine)*

la	**caviglia**	ankle
la	**faccia** *(pl-ce)*	face
la	**fronte**	forehead
la	**guancia** *(pl-ce)*	cheek
la	**lingua**	tongue
le	**orecchie**	ears
la	**pelle**	skin
le	**sopracciglia**	eyebrows
la	**spalla**	shoulder
la	**voce**	voice

USEFUL PHRASES

grande big
alto(a) tall
piccolo(a) small
basso(a) short
grasso(a) fat
magro(a) skinny
snello(a) slim
bello(a) beautiful; handsome
carino(a) pretty; cute
brutto(a) ugly

USEFUL WORDS *(masculine)*

il	**cervello**	brain
il	**ciglio** *(pl f ciglia)*	eyelash
il	**dito del piede**	toe
il	**ditone**	the big toe
il	**fegato**	liver
il	**fianco**	hip
il	**gesto**	gesture
il	**gomito**	elbow
un	**indice**	forefinger
il	**labbro** *(pl f labbra)*	lip
i	**lineamenti**	features
il	**muscolo**	muscle
un	**osso** *(pl f ossa)*	bone
il	**polmone**	lung
il	**polpaccio**	calf *(of leg)*
il	**polso**	wrist
il	**pugno**	fist
il	**rene**	kidney
lo	**scheletro**	skeleton
il	**sedere**	bottom
il	**seno**	breast
il	**tallone**	heel
il	**tratto**	feature

USEFUL PHRASES

soffiarsi il naso to blow one's nose
tagliarsi le unghie to cut one's nails
tagliarsi i capelli to have one's hair cut
scrollare le spalle to shrug one's shoulders
fare cenno di sì con il capo to nod one's head *(say yes)*
fare cenno di no con il capo to shake one's head *(say no)*
vedere to see; sentire to hear; to feel
annusare to smell; toccare to touch; assaggiare to taste
stringere la mano a qn to shake hands with sb
salutare qn con la mano to wave at sb
indicare qc to point at sth

USEFUL WORDS *(feminine)*

un'	**anca** *(pl -che)*	hip
un'	**arteria**	artery
la	**carnagione**	skin, complexion
la	**carne**	flesh
le	**ciglia**	eyelashes
la	**colonna vertebrale**	spine
la	**coscia** *(pl -sce)*	thigh
la	**costola**	rib
le	**dita del piede**	toes
la	**fronte**	temple *(of head)*
le	**labbra**	lips
la	**mandibola**	jaw
la	**nuca** *(pl -che)*	nape of the neck
le	**ossa**	bones
la	**palpebra**	eyelid
la	**pianta del piede**	sole of the foot
la	**pupilla**	pupil *(of the eye)*
la	**taglia**	size
un'	**unghia**	nail
la	**vena**	vein
la	**vita**	waist

USEFUL PHRASES

(misura dei) fianchi hip measurement

giro vita waist measurement

(misura del) petto chest measurement

sordo(a) deaf

cieco(a) blind

muto(a) mute

disabile disabled

persona con difficoltà d'apprendimento person with learning difficulties

lui è più alto di te he is taller than you

Sara è cresciuta molto Sara has grown a lot

sono in sovrappeso I am overweight

è ingrassata/dimagrita she has put on weight/lost weight

è alta 1 metro e 47 she is 1.47 metres tall

pesa 40 chili he/she weighs 40 kilos

SEASONS

la	**primavera**	spring
l'	**estate** (f)	summer
l'	**autunno** (m)	autumn
l'	**inverno** (m)	winter

MONTHS

gennaio	January	**luglio**	July
febbraio	February	**agosto**	August
marzo	March	**settembre**	September
aprile	April	**ottobre**	October
maggio	May	**novembre**	November
giugno	June	**dicembre**	December

DAYS OF THE WEEK

lunedì	Monday
martedì	Tuesday
mercoledì	Wednesday
giovedì	Thursday
venerdì	Friday
sabato	Saturday
domenica	Sunday

USEFUL PHRASES

in primavera/estate/autunno/inverno in spring/summer/autumn/winter
in maggio in May
il 10 luglio 2009 on 10 July 2009
è il 3 dicembre it's 3rd December
di sabato vado in piscina on Saturdays I go to the swimming pool
sabato sono andato in piscina on Saturday I went to the swimming pool
il prossimo sabato/sabato scorso next/last Saturday
il sabato prima/dopo the previous/following Saturday

un	**anno**	year
il	**calendario**	calendar
i	**giorni della settimana**	days of the week
il	**giorno**	day
il	**giorno festivo**	public holiday
il	**mese**	month
la	**settimana**	week
la	**stagione**	season

USEFUL PHRASES

fare ponte to take a long weekend

il primo aprile the first of April, April Fools' Day

il pesce d'aprile April Fools' trick

il primo maggio Labour day

il carnevale carnival period prior to Lent

l'Epifania Epiphany (6 January)

Ferragosto August 15 (Bank Holiday in Italy)

San Valentino St Valentine's Day

Ognissanti All Saints' Day

Pasqua Easter

Domenica di Pasqua Easter Sunday

Pasquetta or Lunedì di Pasqua Easter Monday

Mercoledì delle Ceneri Ash Wednesday

Venerdì Santo Good Friday

la Quaresima Lent

la Pasqua ebraica Passover

il Ramadan Ramadan

Hanukkah Hanukkah or Hanukah

la vigilia di Natale Christmas Eve

Natale Christmas

il giorno di Natale Christmas Day

San Silvestro New Year's Eve

Capodanno New Year's Day; New Year's Eve

il cenone/festa di Capodanno New Year's Eve dinner/party

ESSENTIAL WORDS *(masculine)*

un	**anniversario di matrimonio**	wedding anniversary
un	**appuntamento**	appointment, date
il	**biglietto d'auguri**	greetings card
il	**compleanno**	birthday
il	**divorzio**	divorce
il	**matrimonio**	marriage; wedding
un	**onomastico**	saint's day
il	**regalo**	present

IMPORTANT WORDS *(masculine)*

il	**falò** *(pl inv)*	bonfire
il	**fidanzamento**	engagement
i	**fuochi d'artificio**	fireworks; firework display
il	**parco** *(pl -chi)* **dei divertimenti**	fun fair

USEFUL WORDS *(masculine)*

il	**battesimo**	christening
il	**cimitero**	cemetery
il	**funerale**	funeral
il	**regalo di Natale**	Christmas present
il	**testimone**	witness

USEFUL PHRASES

festeggiare il compleanno to celebrate one's birthday
mia sorella è nata nel 1995 my sister was born in 1995
ha appena compiuto 17 anni he/she has just turned 17
mi ha fatto un regalo he/she gave me a present
te lo regalo! I'm giving it to you!
grazie thank you
divorziare to get divorced
sposarsi to get married
fidanzarsi (con qn) to get engaged (to sb)
mio padre è morto due anni fa my father died two years ago
seppellire to bury

ESSENTIAL WORDS *(feminine)*

la **data**	date
la **festa**	party; birthday
la **morte**	death
la **nascita**	birth
le **nozze**	wedding

IMPORTANT WORDS *(feminine)*

le **feste**	festivities
la **fiera**	fair
la **sagra**	festival

USEFUL WORDS *(feminine)*

la **cerimonia**	ceremony
la **damigella (d'onore)**	bridesmaid
la **luna di miele**	honeymoon
la **participazione (di nozze)**	wedding invitation
la **pensione**	retirement
la **prima comunione**	first communion
la **processione**	procession
la **testimone**	witness

USEFUL PHRASES

nozze d'oro/argento/diamante silver/golden/diamond wedding anniversary

fare gli auguri di Buon Anno a qn to wish sb a happy New Year

dare una festa to have a party

invitare gli amici to invite friends

scegliere un regalo to choose a gift

Buon Natale! Happy Christmas!

Buon compleanno! happy birthday!

auguri best wishes

ESSENTIAL WORDS *(masculine)*

il **bidone della spazzatura**	dustbin
il **campeggiatore**	camper
il **campeggio**	camping; campsite
il **camper** *(pl inv)*	camper van
il **coltello**	knife
il **cucchiaio**	spoon
il **fiammifero**	match
il **gas** *(pl inv)*	gas
il **piatto**	plate
il **picchetto**	tent peg
il **posto**	place; vacancy
i **servizi**	washrooms; toilets
lo **specchio**	mirror
il **supplemento**	extra charge
il **tavolino**	table
il **temperino**	penknife
il **veicolo**	vehicle

IMPORTANT WORDS *(masculine)*

un **apribottiglie** *(pl inv)*	corkscrew
un **apriscatole** *(pl inv)*	tin-opener
il **barbecue** *(pl inv)*	barbecue
il **bucato**	washing
il **detersivo**	washing powder
il **fango** *(pl -ghi)*	mud
il **fornello**	stove
un **igloo** *(pl inv)*	dome tent
il **martello**	hammer
il **materassino gonfiabile**	airbed
il **regolamento**	rules
il **sacco a pelo**	sleeping bag
lo **zaino**	rucksack

USEFUL PHRASES
andare in campeggio to go camping
accamparsi to camp
ben attrezzato(a) well equipped

ESSENTIAL WORDS *(feminine)*

l'	**acqua (non) potabile**	(non-)drinking water
la	**bombola del gas**	gas cylinder
la	**brandina**	camp bed
la	**campeggiatrice**	camper
la	**cassa**	box
la	**doccia** *(pl -ce)*	shower
la	**forchetta**	fork
la	**lattina**	can, tin
la	**lavatrice**	washing machine
la	**notte**	night
la	**piazzola**	pitch, site
la	**pila**	torch, flashlight; battery
la	**piscina**	swimming pool
la	**roulotte** *(pl inv)*	caravan
la	**scatola**	box, tin
la	**(sedia a) sdraio**	deckchair
la	**sedia pieghevole**	folding chair
la	**stanza**	room
la	**tenda (da campeggio)**	tent
le	**toilette**	toilets

IMPORTANT WORDS *(feminine)*

la	**lavanderia**	launderette
l'	**ombra**	shade; shadow
la	**presa di corrente**	socket
la	**sala giochi**	games room

USEFUL PHRASES

montare una tenda to pitch a tent
fare salsicce alla griglia to grill sausages

ESSENTIAL WORDS *(masculine)*

un	agente di polizia	policeman
un	assistente di volo	flight attendant
il	capo	boss
il	carabiniere	policeman
il	cassiere	check-out assistant
il	commercio	trade
il	commesso	sales assistant, shop assistant
il	consulente professionale	careers adviser
il	datore di lavoro	employer
il	dipendente	employee
il	disegnatore di pagine web	web designer
il	dottore	doctor
un	elettricista	electrician
il	farmacista	chemist
un	impiegato	clerk
un	infermiere	nurse
un	ingegnere	engineer
un	insegnante	teacher
il	lavoro	job; work
il	macchinista	train driver
il	meccanico	mechanic
il	medico	doctor
il	poliziotto	policeman
il	pompiere	fireman
il	postino	postman
il	professore	teacher
il	programmatore	computer programmer
il	redattore	editor
il	soldato	soldier
lo	steward *(pl inv)*	steward
un	ufficio	office
il	vigile	traffic warden

USEFUL PHRASES

interessante/poco interessante **interesting/not very interesting**
fa il postino **he is a postman**; fa il medico **he/she is a doctor**
lavorare **to work**; diventare **to become**

ESSENTIAL WORDS *(feminine)*

un'	**ambizione**	ambition
un'	**assistente di volo**	flight attendant
la	**banca**	bank
la	**cassiera**	check-out assistant
la	**commessa**	sales assistant, shop assistant
la	**consulente professionale**	careers adviser
la	**dipendente**	employee
la	**dottoressa**	doctor
la	**fabbrica** *(pl -che)*	factory
la	**hostess** *(pl inv)*	stewardess
un'	**impiegata**	clerk
un'	**infermiera**	nurse
un'	**insegnante**	teacher
la	**paga**	wages
la	**pensione**	retirement
la	**postina**	postwoman
la	**professione**	profession
la	**professoressa**	teacher
la	**programmatrice**	computer programmer
la	**receptionist** *(pl inv)*	receptionist
la	**redattrice**	editor
la	**segretaria**	secretary
la	**star** *(m+f pl inv)*	film star
la	**vita**	life
la	**vita lavorativa**	working life

USEFUL PHRASES

lavorare per guadagnarsi da vivere to work for one's living
che lavoro fa? what do you do (for a living)?
cosa vuoi fare da grande? what do you want to do when you grow up?
fare domanda di lavoro to apply for a job

IMPORTANT WORDS *(masculine)*

gli	**affari**	business
l'	**apprendistato**	apprenticeship
un	**aumento**	rise
un	**autore**	author
il	**barbiere**	barber
il	**bidello**	caretaker, janitor *(at school)*
il	**collega** *(pl -ghi)*	colleague
il	**commerciante**	shopkeeper
il	**contratto**	contract
il	**cuoco** *(pl -chi)*	cook
il	**custode**	caretaker *(of building)*
il	**dirigente**	manager
il	**disoccupato**	unemployed person
il	**futuro**	future
un	**idraulico**	plumber
un	**imbianchino**	decorator
un	**impiego** *(pl -ghi)*	job; situation
un	**interinale**	temp
il	**lavoratore**	worker
il	**manager** *(pl inv)*	manager
il	**mercato del lavoro**	job market
un	**operaio**	worker
un	**ottico**	optician
il	**parrucchiere**	hairdresser
il	**pilota**	pilot
il	**pittore**	painter
il	**pompiere**	fireman
il	**posto di lavoro**	job
il	**presidente**	president; chairperson
lo	**sciopero**	strike
il	**sindacato**	trade union
un	**uomo d'affari**	businessman

USEFUL PHRASES

essere disoccupato(a) to be unemployed
licenziare qn per eccesso di personale to make sb redundant
un contratto a tempo indeterminato a permanent contract
un contratto a tempo determinato temporary contract

IMPORTANT WORDS *(feminine)*

un'	**agenzia di collocamento**	job centre
un'	**agenzia di lavoro temporaneo**	temping agency
la	**biblioteca** *(pl -che)*	library
la	**bidella**	caretaker, janitor *(at school)*
la	**carriera**	career
la	**collega** *(pl -ghi)*	colleague
la	**cuoca** *(pl -che)*	cook
la	**custode**	caretaker *(of building)*
la	**dirigente**	manager
la	**disoccupazione**	unemployment
la	**domanda**	application
la	**donna d'affari**	businesswoman
la	**donna delle pulizie**	cleaner
un'	**interinale**	temp
la	**lettera d'accompagnamento**	covering letter
la	**manager** *(pl inv)*	manager
un'	**operaia**	worker
la	**parrucchiera**	hairdresser
la	**pittrice**	painter
la	**politica**	politics
la	**presidente**	president; chairperson

USEFUL PHRASES

"domande di impiego" **"situations wanted"**
"offerte di impiego" **"situations vacant"**
appartenere ad un sindacato **to be in a union**
guadagnare 1000 euro al mese **to earn 1000 euros per month**
un aumento (di paga) **a pay rise**
scioperare *or* fare sciopero **to go on strike**
essere in sciopero **to be on strike**
lavorare a tempo pieno/lavorare part-time **to work full-time/to work part-time**
fare lo straordinario **to work overtime**
riduzione delle ore lavorative **reduction in working hours**

USEFUL WORDS *(masculine)*

un	agricoltore	farmer *(crops)*
un	allevatore	farmer *(animals)*
un	architetto	architect
un	artista	artist
un	avvocato	lawyer; solicitor
il	chirurgo *(pl -ghi)*	surgeon
il	colloquio *(di lavoro)*	(job) interview
il	contabile	accountant
il	corso di formazione	training course
il	cosmonauta	cosmonaut
il	deputato	MP
il	direttore amministrativo	company secretary
un	elettrauto	car electrician
il	falegname	joiner, carpenter
il	fotografo	photographer
il	funzionario	civil servant
il	giornalista	journalist
il	giudice	judge
un	ingegnere	engineer
un	interprete	interpreter
il	marinaio	sailor
il	minatore	miner
il	modello	model
il	muratore	bricklayer; mason
il	notaio	notary
il	personale	staff
il	politico	politician
il	prete	priest
il	rappresentante	sales rep
un	ricercatore	researcher
lo	scrittore	writer
lo	stilista	fashion designer
il	sussidio di disoccupazione	unemployment benefit
il	tassista	taxi driver
il	tirocinio	apprenticeship; training
il	traduttore	translator
il	veterinario	vet
il	viticoltore	wine grower

USEFUL WORDS *(feminine)*

un'	agente di polizia	policewoman
un'	amministrazione	administration
un'	annunciatrice	announcer
un'	artista	artist
la	casalinga *(pl -ghe)*	housewife, home maker
la	cassa integrazione	redundancy payment
la	contabile	accountant
la	deputata	MP
la	direttrice amministrativa	company secretary
la	ditta	business
la	formazione	training
la	giornalista	journalist
un'	impresa	company; business
un'	interprete	interpreter
la	modella	model
la	monaca *(pl -che)*	nun
la	poliziotta	policewoman
la	rappresentante	rep; sales rep
la	sarta	dressmaker
la	società *(pl inv)*	company
la	suora	nun
la	traduttrice	translator
la	vigile	traffic warden

USEFUL PHRASES

un lavoro stagionale seasonal work

un lavoro temporaneo/fisso a temporary/permanent job

un lavoro part-time a part-time job

essere assunto(a) to be taken on; essere licenziato(a) to be dismissed

licenziare qn to give sb the sack

cercare lavoro to look for work

fare un corso di formazione professionale to go on a training course

timbrare il cartellino to clock in/out

lavorare con un orario flessibile to work flexi-time

ESSENTIAL WORDS *(masculine)*

l'	**acceleratore**	accelerator
un	**agente di polizia**	policeman
un	**autista**	driver; chauffeur
un	**autovelox** *(pl inv)*	speed camera
il	**box** *(pl inv)*	garage *(for parking car)*
il	**cambio**	gear, gearbox
il	**chilometro**	kilometre
il	**ciclista**	cyclist
il	**distributore di benzina**	filling station; petrol pump
i	**fari**	headlights
il	**freno**	brake
il	**garage** *(pl inv)*	garage *(for parking car)*
il	**gasolio**	diesel
il	**guidatore**	driver
un	**incrocio**	crossroads
un	**ingorgo** *(pl -ghi)*	traffic jam
il	**libretto di circolazione**	(car) registration document
il	**litro**	litre
il	**meccanico**	mechanic
il	**motore**	engine
il	**numero**	number
l'	**olio**	oil
il	**parcheggio**	car park
il	**pedaggio**	toll
il	**pedone**	pedestrian
lo	**pneumatico**	tyre
il	**semaforo**	traffic lights
lo	**svincolo autostradale**	motorway exit, junction
il	**viaggio**	journey

USEFUL PHRASES

frenare bruscamente to brake suddenly

100 chilometri all'ora 100 kilometres an hour

ha la patente? do you have a driving licence?

andiamo a fare un giro (in macchina) we're going for a drive (in the car)

ESSENTIAL WORDS *(feminine)*

l'	**acqua**	water
un'	**assicurazione**	insurance
un'	**autista**	driver; chauffeur
un'	**autorimessa**	garage *(for repairs)*
un'	**autostrada**	motorway
la	**benzina**	petrol
la	**benzina senza piombo**	unleaded petrol
la	**carta stradale**	street map
la	**deviazione**	diversion
la	**direzione**	direction
la	**distanza**	distance
la	**gomma**	tyre
la	**guidatrice**	driver
le	**indicazioni**	directions
la	**macchina**	car
la	**patente**	driving licence
la	**polizia**	police
la	**polizza di assicurazione**	insurance policy
la	**roulotte** *(pl inv)*	caravan
la	**stazione di servizio**	service station
la	**strada**	road
la	**strada principale**	main road
la	**strada statale**	main road; A road
la	**targa** *(pl -ghe)*	number plate
un'	**uscita (autostradale)**	motorway exit, junction

USEFUL PHRASES

il pieno, per favore **fill it up please**
prendere la strada per Lecco **to take the road to Lecco**
è un viaggio di tre ore **it's a 3-hour journey**
buon viaggio! **have a good journey!**
andiamo! **let's go!**
lungo la strada abbiamo visto ... **on the way we saw ...**
sorpassare una macchina **to overtake a car**

IMPORTANT WORDS *(masculine)*

un	**autolavaggio**	car wash
un	**automobilista**	motorist
l'	**autostop**	hitch-hiking
un	**autostoppista**	hitch-hiker
il	**bagagliaio**	boot
il	**benzinaio**	petrol pump attendant
il	**camionista**	lorry driver
il	**carro attrezzi**	breakdown van
il	**cartello stradale**	road sign
il	**clacson** *(pl inv)*	horn
il	**codice della strada**	highway code
il	**confine**	border
il	**cruscotto**	dashboard
il	**danno**	damage
i	**documenti (della macchina)**	official papers
il	**faro**	headlight
il	**guasto**	breakdown
un	**incidente (stradale)**	(road) accident
il	**motociclista**	motorcyclist
il	**parcheggio**	parking
il	**pezzo di ricambio**	spare part
lo	**scontro**	collision
il	**traffico**	traffic

USEFUL PHRASES

accendere il motore **to switch on the engine**
il motore parte **the engine starts up**
il motore non parte **the engine won't start**
accelerare **to accelerate**; proseguire **to continue**
ridurre la velocità **to slow down**
fermarsi **to stop**; parcheggiare (la macchina) **to park (the car)**
spegnere il motore **to switch off the engine**
fermarsi con il semaforo rosso **to stop at the red light**

IMPORTANT WORDS *(feminine)*

un'	**automobile**	car
un'	**automobilista**	motorist
un'	**autoscuola**	driving school
un'	**autostoppista**	hitch-hiker
la	**batteria**	battery
la	**carrozzeria**	body work
la	**cintura di sicurezza**	seat belt
la	**collisione**	collision
la	**foratura**	puncture
la	**frizione**	clutch
la	**marca** *(pl -che)*	make *(of car)*
la	**marcia** *(pl -ce)*	gear
la	**motociclista**	motorcyclist
la	**pompa di benzina**	petrol pump
la	**portiera**	(car) door
la	**prova del palloncino**	Breathalyser® test
la	**revisione**	MOT test
la	**rotatoria**	roundabout
la	**rotonda**	roundabout
la	**ruota di scorta**	spare tyre
la	**scuola guida**	driving school
la	**strada a senso unico**	one-way street
la	**velocità**	speed
la	**zona a traffico limitato**	controlled traffic zone
la	**zona pedonale**	pedestrian zone

USEFUL PHRASES

c'è stato un incidente there's been an accident

nell'incidente sono rimaste ferite sei persone six people were injured in the accident

favorisce i documenti, per cortesia? may I see your papers please?

forare to have a puncture; riparare to fix

avere un'avaria to break down

sono rimasto senza benzina I've run out of petrol

USEFUL WORDS *(masculine)*

il **carabiniere**	policeman
il **carburatore**	carburettor
il **catalizzatore**	catalytic converter
il **centro abitato**	built-up area
il **certificato di assicurazione**	insurance certificate
il **cofano**	bonnet
il **consumo di benzina**	petrol consumption
il **contachilometri** *(pl inv)*	speedometer
un **istruttore di guida**	driving instructor
il **lavaggio auto**	car-wash
il **limite di velocità**	speed limit
il **navigatore satellitare**	satellite navigation system (satnav)
il **parabrezza** *(pl inv)*	windscreen
il **paraurti** *(pl inv)*	bumper
il **parchimetro**	parking meter
il **pedale**	pedal
il **portapacchi** *(pl inv)*	roof rack
il **principiante**	learner driver
il **pulsante di avvio**	starter
il **rimorchio**	trailer
il **servosterzo**	power steering
il **(sistema di navigazione) GPS**	satellite navigation system
lo **spartitraffico** *(pl inv)*	central reservation
lo **specchietto retrovisore**	rear-view mirror
il **tergicristalli** *(pl inv)*	windscreen wiper
il **vigile**	traffic warden
il **volante**	steering wheel

USEFUL PHRASES

a rimorchio on tow

nell'ora di punta at rush hour

ha ricevuto una multa di 100 euro he got a 100-euro fine

è assicurato? are you insured?

non dimentichi di allacciare le cinture di sicurezza don't forget to put on
  your seat belts

al confine at the border

fare l'autostop to hitch-hike

USEFUL WORDS *(feminine)*

un'	area di servizio	service station
la	rampa d'accesso	slip road
la	circonvallazione	ring road
la	corsia	lane
la	corsia d'emergenza	hard shoulder
la	curva	bend
la	deviazione	detour
la	freccia *(pl -ce)*	indicator
la	frenata improvvisa	emergency stop
un'	infrazione stradale	traffic offence
la	lezione di guida	driving lesson
la	multa	fine
la	piazzola di sosta	lay-by
la	pressione	pressure
la	stazione di servizio	service station
la	via	street
la	vigile	traffic warden
la	vittima	casualty

USEFUL PHRASES

la ruota anteriore/posteriore the front/back wheel
dobbiamo fare una deviazione we have to make a detour
una multa per eccesso di velocità a fine for speeding
accosti per favore pull in please
"dare la precedenza" "give way to the right"
"tenere la destra" "keep to the right"
"vietato l'accesso" "no entry"
"divieto di sosta" "no parking"
"lavori in corso" "roadworks"

ESSENTIAL WORDS (*masculine*)

l'	abito	suit; dress
il	bottone	button
il	calzino	sock
i	calzoni	trousers
il	cappello	hat
il	cappotto	coat
i	collant	tights
il	costume da bagno	swimming trunks; swimsuit
il	fazzoletto	handkerchief
un	impermeabile	raincoat
i	jeans	jeans
il	maglione	jumper
il	numero (di scarpe)	(shoe) size
un	ombrello	umbrella
i	pantaloncini	shorts
i	pantaloni	trousers
il	pigiama	pyjamas
il	reggiseno	bra
gli	slip (*pl inv*)	knickers; underpants
il	soprabito	overcoat
i	vestiti	clothes
il	vestito	suit; dress; costume

IMPORTANT WORDS (*masculine*)

un	accappatoio	bathrobe
il	cappuccio	hood
il	giaccone	heavy jacket
il	golf (*pl inv*)	cardigan
il	guanto	glove
i	pantaloni corti	shorts
il	sandalo	sandal
lo	scarpone	boot
gli	shorts	shorts
gli	stivali	boots

ESSENTIAL WORDS *(feminine)*

la	biancheria intima	underwear
la	borsa	bag
la	borsetta	handbag
la	camicia	shirt
la	camicia da notte	nightdress
la	cravatta	tie
la	felpa	sweatshirt
la	giacca *(pl -che)*	jacket
la	giacca *(pl -che)* a vento	anorak
la	gonna	skirt
la	maglietta	T-shirt
la	moda	fashion
le	mutande	underpants; knickers
la	scarpa	shoe
la	taglia	size
la	vita	waist

IMPORTANT WORDS *(feminine)*

la	blusa	blouse
la	canottiera	vest
la	ciabatta	slipper
la	cintura	belt
la	roba da vestire	clothes
la	tasca	pocket
un'	uniforme	uniform
la	vestaglia	dressing gown

USEFUL PHRASES

di mattina mi vesto in the morning I get dressed
di sera mi spoglio in the evening I get undressed
quando torno a casa da scuola mi cambio when I get home from school I
   get changed
indossare *or* avere addosso to wear
mettersi to put on
è molto elegante that's very smart

USEFUL WORDS (*masculine*)

gli	**accessori**	accessories
il	**bastone (da passeggio)**	walking stick
i	**bermuda**	Bermuda shorts
il	**berretto**	cap; beret
il	**bucato**	washing
il	**camice**	overalls
il	**colletto**	collar
il	**fiocco** (*pl* -chi)	bow
il	**foulard** (*pl inv*)	scarf
il	**gilè** (*pl inv*)	waistcoat
il	**grembiule**	apron
gli	**infradito**	flip flops
i	**lacci**	(shoe)laces
il	**nastro**	ribbon
un	**occhiello**	buttonhole
il	**papillon** (*pl inv*)	bow tie
lo	**spogliatoio**	changing room
il	**vestito da sera**	evening dress
il	**vestito da sposa**	wedding dress

USEFUL PHRASES

ti sta bene that suits you

che taglia porti (*or* porta)? what size do you take?

che numero di scarpe porti (*or* porta)? what shoe size do you take?

ho il 38 di piede I take size 38 in shoes

USEFUL WORDS *(feminine)*

l'	**alta moda**	haute couture
la	**(borsa a) tracolla**	shoulder bag
le	**bretelle**	braces
le	**calze**	stockings; socks
la	**canotta**	tank top
la	**chiusura lampo** *(pl -e ~)*	zip
la	**felpa**	sweatshirt
la	**gonna pantalone**	culottes
la	**maglia con il cappuccio**	hooded top
la	**maglietta senza maniche**	tank top
la	**manica** *(pl -che)*	sleeve
la	**polo** *(pl inv)*	polo shirt
la	**pulitura a secco**	dry-cleaning
la	**salopette** *(pl inv)*	dungarees
le	**scarpe basse**	flat shoes
le	**scarpe con i tacchi**	high heels
le	**scarpe da ginnastica**	trainers
la	**sfilata di moda**	fashion show
la	**sottogonna**	underskirt
la	**tuta da ginnastica**	tracksuit
la	**zip** *(pl inv)*	zip

USEFUL PHRASES

lungo(a) **long**; corto(a) **short**
un vestito con le maniche corte/lunghe **a short-sleeved/long-sleeved dress**
stretto(a) **tight**
largo(a) **loose**
una gonna attillata **a tight skirt**
a strisce **striped**; a quadretti **checked**; a pallini **spotted**
vestiti sportivi **casual clothes**
in pigiama **in pyjamas**
alla moda **fashionable**; moderno(a) **trendy**
fuori moda **old-fashioned**

arancione	orange
azzurro(a)	light blue
beige *(pl inv)*	beige
bianco(a)	white
blu *(pl inv)*	blue
blu marina *(pl inv)*	navy blue
blu scuro *(pl inv)*	dark blue
bordeaux *(pl inv)*	maroon
celeste	sky blue
d'argento *(pl inv)*	silver
dorato(a)	golden
d'oro *(pl inv)*	gold
giallo(a)	yellow
grigio(a)	grey
malva *(pl inv)*	mauve
marrone	brown
naturale	natural
nero(a)	black
rosa *(pl inv)*	pink
rosso(a)	red
rosso fuoco *(pl inv)*	bright red
turchese	turquoise
verde	green
viola *(pl inv)*	purple
violetto(a)	violet

USEFUL PHRASES

il colore colour

di che colore hai (*or* ha) gli occhi/i capelli? what colour are your eyes/is your
hair?

il blu ti sta bene blue suits you

quello blu ti sta bene the blue one suits you

dipingere qc di blu to paint sth blue

le scarpe blu blue shoes

le scarpe azzurre light blue shoes

ha gli occhi verdi she/he has green eyes

cambiare colore to change colour

la Casa Bianca the White House

un (uomo) bianco a white man

una (donna) bianca a white woman

un (uomo) nero a black man

una (donna) nera a black woman

bianco come la neve as white as snow

Biancaneve Snow White

Cappuccetto Rosso Little Red Riding Hood

diventare rosso(a) to turn red, to blush

rosso(a) come un peperone as red as a beetrot

chiaro(a)/scuro(a) light/dark

nero(a) come il carbone as brown as a berry

un occhio nero a black eye

un (romanzo) giallo a crime novel

un romanzo rosa a romantic novel

Pagine Gialle Yellow pages

una notte in bianco a sleepless night

riso/pasta in bianco plain rice/pasta

la benzina verde unleaded petrol

numero verde freephone

essere al verde to be broke

essere di umore nero to be in a very bad mood

ESSENTIAL WORDS (masculine)

il	computer (pl inv)	computer
il	mouse (pl inv)	mouse
il	programma	program

USEFUL WORDS (masculine)

l'	ADSL	broadband
il	backup (pl inv)	back-up
il	browser (pl inv)	browser
il	CD-ROM (pl inv)	CD-ROM
il	computer fisso	desktop computer
il	correttore ortografico	spellchecker
il	cursore	cursor
il	data base (pl inv)	database
i	dati	data
il	disco esterno (pl -chi -i)	external disk
il	disco rigido	hard disk
il	documento	document
il	file (pl inv)	file
il	foglio di calcolo	spreadsheet
il	gioco per il computer	computer game
un	indirizzo di posta elettronica	e-mail address
	Internet	internet
il	lettore DVD	DVD player
il	masterizzatore DVD	DVD writer
il	menu (pl inv)	menu
il	messaggio di posta elettronica	email message
il	modem (pl inv)	modem
il	monitor (pl inv)	monitor
il	navigatore internet	internet user
il	pirata informatico	hacker
il	portatile	laptop
il	router wifi (pl inv)	wifi router
lo	schermo	screen
il	sito web	website
il	software (pl inv)	software
il	tasto	key (on keyboard)
il	virus (pl inv)	virus
il	Web	Web

ESSENTIAL WORDS *(feminine)*

l' **informatica**	computer science; computer studies
la **stampante**	printer

USEFUL WORDS *(feminine)*

un' **applicazione**	program
la **banda larga**	broadband
la **cartuccia d'inchiostro**	ink cartridge
la **chiavetta USB**	USB key
la **copia di sicurezza**	back-up
la **finestra**	window
la **funzione**	function
la **home page** *(pl inv)*	home page
un' **icona**	icon
un' **interfaccia** *(pl -ce)*	interface
la **mail** *(pl inv)*	email (message)
la **memoria**	memory
la **(memoria) RAM**	RAM, random-access memory
la **(memoria) ROM**	ROM, read-only Memory
la **navigatrice internet**	internet user
la **password** *(pl inv)*	password
la **posta elettronica**	email
la **rete**	network
la **scheda di memoria**	memory stick
la **stampa**	print-out
la **tastiera**	keyboard
un' **unità disco** *(pl inv)*	disk drive
la **webcam** *(pl inv)*	webcam

USEFUL PHRASES

copiare to copy; cancellare to delete
formattare to format
scaricare/caricare un file to download/upload a file
salvare to save; stampare to print; digitare to key
visualizzare to view
navigare in Internet to surf the internet

ESSENTIAL WORDS (*masculine*)

il	Belgio	Belgium
il	Canada	Canada
il	Galles	Wales
il	paese	country; village
i	Paesi Bassi	Netherlands
il	Regno Unito	United Kingdom
gli	Stati Uniti	United States
il	Sudamerica	South America
gli	USA	USA

USEFUL WORDS (*masculine*)

il	Brasile	Brazil
El	Salvador	El Salvador
il	Giappone	Japan
il	Marocco	Morocco
il	Messico	Mexico
il	Pakistan	Pakistan
il	Perù	Peru
il	Terzo Mondo	Third World

USEFUL PHRASES

il mio paese d'origine my native country
la capitale italiana the capital of Italy
di che paese sei? what country do you come from?
sono italiano/canadese I am Italian/Canadian
sono nato in Scozia I was born in Scotland
vado nei Paesi Bassi I'm going to the Netherlands
sono appena tornato dagli Stati Uniti I've just come back from the United States
sei mai stato in Italia? have you ever been to Italy?
i paesi in via di sviluppo the developing countries
i paesi di lingua spagnola Spanish-speaking countries

ESSENTIAL WORDS *(feminine)*

l'	**America**	America
l'	**Europa**	Europe
la	**Francia**	France
la	**Germania**	Germany
la	**Gran Bretagna**	Great Britain
l'	**Inghilterra**	England
l'	**Irlanda (del Nord)**	(Northern) Ireland
l'	**Italia**	Italy
l'	**Olanda**	Holland
la	**Scozia**	Scotland
la	**Spagna**	Spain
la	**Svizzera**	Switzerland

USEFUL WORDS *(feminine)*

l'	**Africa**	Africa
l'	**Algeria**	Algeria
l'	**America del sud**	South America
l'	**Asia**	Asia
l'	**Australia**	Australia
l'	**Austria**	Austria
la	**Cina**	China
la	**Croazia**	Croatia
la	**Finlandia**	Finland
la	**Grecia**	Greece
l'	**India**	India
la	**Norvegia**	Norway
la	**Nuova Zelanda**	New Zealand
la	**Russia**	Russia
la	**Slovenia**	Slovenia
la	**Tunisia**	Tunisia
l'	**Ungheria**	Hungary
l'	**Unione europea, la UE**	the European Union, the EU

ESSENTIAL WORDS *(masculine)*

un	**americano**	an American
un	**belga**	a Belgian
un	**britannico**	a Briton
un	**canadese**	a Canadian
un	**europeo**	a European
un	**francese**	a Frenchman
un	**gallese**	a Welshman
un	**inglese**	an Englishman
un	**irlandese**	an Irishman
un	**italiano**	an Italian
un	**olandese**	a Dutchman
un	**pachistano**	a Pakistani
uno	**scozzese**	a Scot
uno	**spagnolo**	a Spaniard
uno	**svizzero**	a Swiss (man *or* boy)
un	**tedesco** (*pl* -chi)	a German
un	**ungherese**	a Hungarian

USEFUL PHRASES

è irlandese he/she is Irish
la campagna irlandese the Irish countryside
una città irlandese an Irish town

ESSENTIAL WORDS *(feminine)*

un'	**americana**	an American
una	**belga**	a Belgian
una	**britannica** *(pl -che)*	a Briton, a British woman *or* girl
una	**canadese**	a Canadian
un'	**europea**	a European
una	**francese**	a Frenchwoman, a French girl
una	**gallese**	a Welshwoman, a Welsh girl
un'	**inglese**	an Englishwoman, an English girl
un'	**irlandese**	an Irishwoman, an Irish girl
un'	**italiana**	an Italian
un'	**olandese**	a Dutchwoman, a Dutch girl
una	**pachistana**	a Pakistani
una	**scozzese**	a Scot
una	**spagnola**	a Spaniard
una	**svizzera**	a Swiss woman *or* girl
una	**tedesca** *(pl -che)*	a German
un'	**ungherese**	a Hungarian

USEFUL PHRASES

parlo inglese **I speak English**
sono scozzese **I am Scottish**
uno(a) straniero(a) **a foreigner**
all'estero **abroad**
la nazionalità **nationality**

USEFUL WORDS *(masculine)*

un	**africano**	an African
un	**albanese**	an Albanian
un	**arabo**	an Arab
un	**argentino**	an Argentinian
un	**asiatico** *(pl -chi)*	an Asian
un	**australiano**	an Australian
un	**caraibico** *(pl -chi)*	a West Indian
un	**ceco** *(pl -chi)*	a Czech
un	**cinese**	a Chinese
un	**giapponese**	a Japanese
un	**indiano**	an Indian
un	**neozelandese**	a New Zealander
un	**portoghese**	a Portuguese
un	**polacco** *(pl -chi)*	a Pole
un	**russo**	a Russian
un	**slovacco** *(pl -chi)*	a Slovakian
un	**turco** *(pl -chi)*	a Turk
un	**ucraino**	a Ukranian

USEFUL WORDS *(feminine)*

un'	**africana**	an African
un'	**albanese**	an Albanian
un'	**araba**	an Arab
un'	**argentina**	an Argentinian
un'	**asiatica** *(pl -che)*	an Asian
un'	**australiana**	an Australian
una	**caraibica** *(pl -che)*	a West Indian
una	**ceca** *(pl -che)*	a Czech
una	**cinese**	a Chinese
una	**giapponese**	a Japanese
un'	**indiana**	an Indian
una	**neozelandese**	a New Zealander
una	**polacca** *(pl -che)*	a Pole
una	**portoghese**	a Portuguese
una	**russa**	a Russian
una	**slovacca** *(pl -che)*	a Slovakian
una	**turca** *(pl -che)*	a Turk
un'	**ucraina**	a Ukranian

ESSENTIAL WORDS *(masculine)*

un	albero	tree
un	allevatore	farmer *(raising animals)*
il	bastone (da passeggio)	walking stick
il	bosco *(pl -chi)*	wood; forest
il	cacciatore	hunter
il	campo	field
il	cancello	gate
il	castello	castle
il	contadino	farmer *(growing crops)*
il	fiume	river
il	furgone	van
il	mercato	market
un	ostello della gioventù	youth hostel
il	paesaggio	scenery
il	paese	village
il	picnic *(pl inv)*	picnic
il	ponte	bridge
il	prato	meadow
il	rifugio	mountain hostel
il	rumore	noise
il	ruscello	stream
il	sasso	stone, pebble
il	sentiero	path; track
lo	steccato	fence
il	suolo	ground
il	terreno	land; ground
il	turista	tourist

USEFUL PHRASES

all'aria aperta in the open air
so come arrivare al paese I know the way to the village
andare in bicicletta to go cycling
gli abitanti del posto the locals
siamo andati a fare un picnic we went for a picnic

ESSENTIAL WORDS *(feminine)*

un'	allevatrice	farmer *(raising animals)*
l'	aria	air
la	cacciatrice	hunter
la	campagna	country; countryside
la	contadina	farmer *(growing crops)*
un'	escursione	hike
la	fattoria	farm, farmhouse
la	montagna	mountain
la	passeggiata	walk
la	pietra	stone
la	regione	district
la	roccia *(pl -ce)*	rock
la	strada	way; road
la	terra	land; earth; soil; ground
la	torre	tower
la	turista	tourist
la	valle	valley

USEFUL PHRASES

in campagna **in the country**
andare in campagna **to go into the country**
vivere in campagna/in città **to live in the country/in town**
coltivare la terra **to cultivate the land**

IMPORTANT WORDS (*masculine*)

il	fienile	barn
il	fiore	flower
il	lago (*pl* -ghi)	lake
il	podere	farm; holding
gli	stivali di gomma	(wellington) boots
il	vigneto	vineyard

USEFUL WORDS (*masculine*)

un	agriturismo	farm where you can have holiday
un	arbusto	bush
il	bastone	stick
il	binocolo	binoculars
il	borgo	hamlet
il	cartello segnaletico	signpost
il	cespuglio	bush
il	ciottolo	pebble
il	fango	mud
il	fieno	hay
il	fossato	ditch
il	furgone	van
il	grano	grain; wheat
il	mulino (a vento)	(wind)mill
il	palo della luce	telegraph pole
il	pozzo	well
il	prato	meadow
il	raccolto	crop; harvest
lo	stagno	pond

USEFUL PHRASES

agricolo(a) agricultural
tranquillo(a) peaceful
in cima alla collina at the top of the hill
cadere in trappola to fall into a trap

IMPORTANT WORDS *(feminine)*

l'	agricoltura	agriculture
la	cima	top *(of hill)*
la	collina	hill
la	foglia	leaf
la	gente di campagna	country people
la	pace	peace, tranquillity
la	polvere	dust
la	proprietà	property; estate
la	stalla	stable
la	tranquillità	tranquillity, peace
la	trattoria	restaurant *(in country)*
la	vigna	vineyard
la	vista	view

USEFUL WORDS *(feminine)*

la	brughiera	moor
la	caccia	hunting
la	cascata	waterfall
la	cava	quarry
l'	erica *(pl -che)*	heather
la	fonte	spring; source
la	grotta	cave
la	palude	marsh
la	pianura	plain
la	pozzanghera	puddle
la	riva	bank *(of river)*
le	rovine	ruins
la	siepe	hedge
la	trappola	trap
la	vendemmia	grape harvest

USEFUL PHRASES

perdersi to lose one's way; to get lost
raccogliere frutta, grano to harvest fruit, grain
vendemmiare, fare la vendemmia to harvest the grapes

ESSENTIAL WORDS *(masculine)*

un	aspetto	appearance
i	baffi	moustache
i	capelli	hair
il	colore	colour
gli	occhi	eyes

USEFUL PHRASES

allegro(a) cheerful
alto(a) tall
antipatico(a) unpleasant
basso(a) short
bello handsome; bella beautiful *(person)*
beneducato(a) well-behaved
brutto(a) ugly
buono(a) kind
calvo(a) bald
carino(a) pretty; cute
cattivo(a) naughty
con la barba bearded, with a beard
dinamico(a) dynamic
divertente amusing, entertaining; funny
educato(a) polite
felice happy
giovane young
grasso(a) fat
infelice unhappy
inquieto(a) agitated
intelligente intelligent
lungo(a) long
magro(a) thin
maleducato(a) rude
nervoso(a) nervous
orribile hideous

ESSENTIAL WORDS *(feminine)*

la	**barba**	beard
l'	**età**	age
l'	**identità**	identity
gli	**occhiali**	glasses
la	**persona**	person
la	**pettinatura**	hairstyle
la	**statura**	height
la	**taglia**	size

USEFUL PHRASES

ottimista/pessimista optimistic/pessimistic
piccolo(a) small, little
serio(a) serious
sfortunato(a) unfortunate
simpatico(a) nice
snello(a) slim
stupendo(a) great
stupido(a) stupid
teso(a) tense
timido(a) shy
tranquillo(a) calm
vecchio(a) old
ha un'aria triste he/she looks sad
stava piangendo he/she was crying
stava sorridendo he/she was smiling
aveva le lacrime agli occhi he/she had tears in his eyes
un uomo di statura media a man of average height
sono alto 1 metro e 70 *or* uno e settanta I am 1 metre 70 tall
di che colore hai (*or* ha) gli occhi/i capelli? what colour are your eyes/is your hair?
ho i capelli chiari I have fair hair
ho gli occhi azzurri/verdi I have blue/green eyes
capelli castano chiaro light brown hair; capelli ricci curly hair; con i capelli rossi red-haired
capelli neri/grigi black/grey hair
capelli scuri/castani dark/brown hair
capelli tinti dyed hair

IMPORTANT WORDS *(masculine)*

il **brufolo**	spot; pimple
il **carattere**	character; nature
lo **sguardo**	look
il **sorriso**	smile
l' **umore**	mood

USEFUL WORDS *(masculine)*

il **difetto**	fault
il **foruncolo**	spot, zit; boil
il **gesto**	gesture
il **gigante**	giant
il **neo**	mole, beauty spot
il **peso**	weight
il **ricciolo**	curl

USEFUL PHRASES

ha un buon carattere he/she is goodnatured
avere la carnagione chiara to have a pale complexion
portare gli occhiali to wear glasses
portare le lenti a contatto to wear contact lenses

IMPORTANT WORDS *(feminine)*

un'	**abitudine**	habit
la	**bellezza**	beauty
la	**bruttezza**	ugliness
la	**carnagione**	complexion
la	**curiosità**	curiosity
un'	**espressione**	expression
le	**lenti a contatto**	contact lenses
la	**qualità**	(good) quality
la	**vita**	waist
la	**voce**	voice

USEFUL WORDS *(feminine)*

la	**cicatrice**	scar
la	**dentiera**	false teeth
la	**fossetta**	dimple
la	**frangia**	fringe
le	**lentiggini**	freckles
la	**permanente**	perm
la	**rassomiglianza**	resemblance
le	**rughe**	wrinkles
la	**timidezza**	shyness

USEFUL PHRASES

sono sempre di buon umore **I am always in a good mood**
è di cattivo umore **he/she is in a bad mood**
si è arrabbiato **he got angry**
assomiglia a sua madre **he/she looks like his/her mother**
si mangia le unghie **he/she bites his/her nails**

ESSENTIAL WORDS *(masculine)*

l'	**alfabeto**	alphabet
un	**alunno**	pupil; schoolboy
un	**amico**	friend
un	**asilo**	nursery school
il	**compagno di classe**	classmate
i	**compiti (per casa)**	homework
il	**compito**	homework; task; test
il	**computer** *(pl inv)*	computer
il	**concerto**	concert
il	**disegno**	drawing
il	**dormitorio**	dormitory
un	**errore**	mistake
un	**esame**	exam
un	**esperimento**	experiment
il	**francese**	French
il	**giorno**	day
il	**gruppo**	group
l'	**inglese**	English
l'	**insegnamento**	education; teaching
l'	**intervallo**	break; playtime
un	**istituto (scolastico)**	school; institute
l'	**italiano**	Italian
il	**laboratorio**	laboratory
i	**lavori manuali**	handicrafts
il	**lavoro**	work
il	**libro**	book
il	**liceo**	secondary school (16 to 18 year olds)
il	**maestro**	primary school teacher
il	**nuoto**	swimming
un	**orario**	timetable
il	**premio**	prize
il	**preside**	headmaster
il	**professore**	teacher
il	**progresso**	progress
il	**quaderno**	exercise book
il	**refettorio**	dining hall

ESSENTIAL WORDS *(feminine)*

un'	**alunna**	pupil; schoolgirl
un'	**amica** *(pl -che)*	friend
un'	**aula**	classroom
la	**biologia**	biology
la	**carta geografica** *(pl -e -che)*	map
la	**chimica**	chemistry
la	**classe**	class; year; classroom
la	**compagna di classe**	school friend
la	**domanda**	question
l'	**educazione fisica**	PE
l'	**elettronica**	electronics
un'	**escursione**	trip; outing
la	**fisica**	physics
la	**frase**	sentence
la	**geografia**	geography
la	**ginnastica**	PE, gymnastics
la	**gomma (da cancellare)**	rubber
l'	**informatica**	computer studies
un'	**interrogazione**	oral test
la	**lavagna**	blackboard
la	**lavagna bianca**	whiteboard
la	**lettura**	reading
la	**lezione**	lesson
le	**lingue straniere**	(modern) languages
la	**maestra**	primary school teacher
la	**matematica**	mathematics, maths
la	**materia (scolastica)**	(school) subject
la	**matita**	pencil
la	**mensa**	canteen
la	**musica**	music
la	**palestra**	gym
la	**parola**	word
la	**penna**	pen
la	**piscina**	swimming pool
la	**presentazione**	presentation
la	**preside**	headmistress
la	**professoressa**	teacher
la	**ricreazione**	break; playtime

ESSENTIAL WORDS *(masculine continued)*

il	**risultato**	result
lo	**sbaglio**	mistake
lo	**scambio**	exchange
lo	**scolaro**	schoolboy
il	**semestre**	semester
lo	**spagnolo**	Spanish
lo	**studente**	student
gli	**studi**	studies
lo	**studio**	study
il	**tedesco**	German
il	**tirocinio**	apprenticeship
il	**voto**	mark

USEFUL PHRASES

lavorare to work
imparare to learn
studiare to study
da quanto tempo studi l'italiano? how long have you been learning Italian?
imparare qc a memoria to learn sth off by heart
ho compiti da fare tutti i giorni I have homework every day
la mia sorellina va alle elementari, io frequento la scuola secondaria my
    little sister goes to primary school – I go to secondary school
insegnare l'italiano to teach Italian
il professore/la professoressa di tedesco the German teacher
ho fatto progressi *or* ho migliorato in matematica I have made progress in
    maths
dare un esame to sit an exam
passare un esame to pass an exam
non passare un esame to fail an exam
essere interrogato(a) to have an oral test
prendere la sufficienza to get a pass mark

ESSENTIAL WORDS *(feminine continued)*

la	**risposta**	answer; reply
la	**sala professori**	staffroom
le	**scienze**	science
la	**scolara**	schoolgirl
la	**scuola**	school
la	**scuola secondaria**	secondary school
la	**scuola (secondaria) superiore**	secondary school *(14 to 19 year olds)*
la	**scuola elementare** *or* **primaria**	primary school
la	**scuola materna**	nursery school
la	**scuola media** *or* **secondaria inferiore**	secondary school *(11 to 14 year olds)*
la	**storia**	history; story
la	**studentessa**	student
un'	**università**	university
le	**vacanze**	holidays
le	**vacanze estive**	summer holidays

USEFUL PHRASES

facile easy; difficile difficult
interessante interesting
noioso(a) boring
leggere to read; scrivere to write
ascoltare to listen (to)
guardare to look at, watch
ripetere to repeat
rispondere to reply
parlare to speak
è la prima *or* la migliore della classe she is top of the class
è la peggiore della classe she is bottom of the class
entrare in classe to go into the classroom
fare un errore *or* uno sbaglio to make a mistake
correggere to correct
ho fatto un errore di grammatica I made a grammatical error
ho ricevuto un bel voto I got a good mark
rispondete alla domanda! answer the question!
alzate la mano! put your hand up!

IMPORTANT WORDS *(masculine)*

un	astuccio portapenne	pencil case
il	certificato	certificate
il	corridoio	corridor
il	cortile (per la ricreazione)	playground
il	diploma	diploma
il	diploma di scuola secondaria	higher school-leaving course/ certificate
un	esame di ammissione	entrance exam
l'	esame di maturità	school-leaving examination
un	esame orale	oral exam
un	esame scritto	written exam
il	foglio di carta	sheet of paper
il	giorno libero	day off
il	regolamento scolastico	school rules
il	righello	ruler
un	ufficio	office
lo	zaino	rucksack; school bag

USEFUL PHRASES

il mio amico sta preparando l'esame di ammissione all'università **my friend is sitting his university entrance exam**

ripassare (la lezione) **to revise**

ripasserò la lezione ancora una volta domani **I'll go over the lesson again tomorrow**

IMPORTANT WORDS *(feminine)*

un'	**assenza**	absence
la	**carta**	paper
la	**cartella**	folder; file; schoolbag
la	**conferenza**	lecture
la	**laurea**	university degree
la	**pagella**	school report
la	**regola**	rule
la	**scuola privata**	private school
la	**scuola statale**	state school
la	**traduzione**	translation

USEFUL PHRASES

al secondo anno **in year two**
al primo anno della scuola media **in year seven**
al secondo anno della scuola media **in year eight**
al terzo anno della scuola media **in year nine**
al primo anno della scuola superiore **in year ten**
al secondo anno della scuola superiore **in year eleven**

presente **present**
assente **absent**
punire un alunno/un'alunna **to punish a pupil**
silenzio! **be quiet!**

USEFUL WORDS *(masculine)*

un	**alunno interno**	boarder
il	**banco** *(pl -chi)*	(pupil's) desk
il	**bidello**	janitor
il	**bloc-notes** *(pl inv)*	jotter
il	**castigo** *(pl -ghi)*	punishment
il	**collegio**	boarding school
il	**comportamento**	behaviour
il	**dizionario**	dictionary
un	**esaminatore**	examiner
un	**esercizio**	exercise
un	**evidenziatore**	highlighter
i	**gabinetti**	lavatories; cloakroom
il	**gesso**	chalk
il	**greco**	Greek
l'	**inchiostro**	ink
un	**insegnante di sostegno**	support teacher
un	**ispettore scolastico**	school inspector
il	**latino**	Latin
il	**libretto delle assenze**	absence sheet
il	**libro di testo**	textbook
il	**liquido correttore**	correction fluid
il	**pennarello**	felt-tip pen
il	**quadrimestre**	term (4 months)
il	**tema**	essay; class exam
il	**temperamatite** *(pl inv)*	pencil sharpener
il	**test** *(pl inv)*	test
il	**trimestre**	term (3 months)
il	**tutor** *(pl inv)*	form tutor
il	**vocabolario**	vocabulary; dictionary

USEFUL WORDS *(feminine)*

un'	alunna interna	boarder
l'	algebra	algebra
l'	aritmetica	arithmetic
la	bidella	janitor
la	biro *(pl inv)*	Biro®
la	brutta copia	rough copy
la	calcolatrice	calculator
la	calligrafia	handwriting
la	cattedra	teacher's desk
la	facoltà *(pl inv)*	faculty
la	fila	row *(of seats etc)*
la	geometria	geometry
la	grammatica	grammar
un'	insegnante di sostegno	support teacher
un'	ispettrice scolastica *(pl -i -che)*	school inspector
la	macchia	blot
l'	ortografia	spelling
la	poesia	poetry; poem
la	prova	test
la	religione	religion; religious education, RE
le	scienze naturali	natural science
la	scuola professionale	technical college
la	somma	sum
la	sufficienza	pass mark; average mark

ESSENTIAL WORDS (masculine)

gli	abitanti	inhabitants
gli	alberi	trees
l'	ambiente	environment
gli	animali	animals
il	bosco (pl -chi)	woods; forest
il	combustibile fossile	fossil fuel
un	ecologista	environmentalist
il	fiore	flower
il	gas (pl inv)	gas
i	gas di scarico	exhaust fumes
il	gasolio	diesel
l'	inquinamento	pollution
il	mare	sea
il	mondo	world
i	pesci	fish
il	tempo	weather; time
i	Verdi	the Greens
il	vetro	glass

IMPORTANT WORDS (masculine)

un	agente inquinante	pollutant
l'	alluminio	aluminium
un	avvenimento	event
il	buco (pl -chi)	hole
il	calore	heat
il	clima	climate
il	danno	damage
il	detersivo	detergent; washing powder
il	fiume	river
il	futuro	future
il	governo	government
il	lago (pl -ghi)	lake
il	pannello solare	solar panel
il	pianeta	planet
il	vegetale	vegetable

ESSENTIAL WORDS *(feminine)*

l'	acqua	water
l'	aria	air
un'	automobile	car
la	benzina	petrol
le	bottiglie	bottles
la	campagna	country
la	carta geografica *(pl -e -che)*	map
la	costa	coast
l'	ecologia	ecology
l'	energia sostenibile	renewable energy
la	fabbrica *(pl -che)*	factory
la	frutta	fruit
un'	isola	island
la	macchina	car
la	montagna	mountain
la	pianta	plant
la	pioggia *(pl -ge)*	rain
la	questione	question
la	regione	region; area
la	specie *(pl inv)*	species
la	spiaggia *(pl -ge)*	beach
la	temperatura	temperature
la	terra	earth; soil; ground
la	verdura	vegetables

IMPORTANT WORDS *(feminine)*

la	centrale eolica *(pl -i -che)*	windfarm
la	centrale nucleare	nuclear plant
la	crisi *(pl inv)*	crisis
la	foresta	forest
la	giungla	jungle
un'	imposta	tax
la	soluzione	solution
la	tassa	tax
la	turbina eolica	wind turbine
la	zona	zone

USEFUL WORDS *(masculine)*

il	**buco dell'ozono**	ozone hole
il	**canale**	canal
i	**CFC (clorofluorocarburi)**	CFCs
i	**cibi biologici**	organic food
il	**combustibile**	fuel
il	**continente**	continent
il	**deserto**	desert
l'	**ecosistema**	ecosystem
il	**fertilizzante**	(artificial) fertilizer
un	**inceneritore**	incinerator
l'	**inquinamento acustico**	noise pollution
un	**oceano**	ocean
un	**OGM (organismo geneticamente modificato)**	GMO
i	**prodotti chimici**	chemicals
il	**prodotto**	product
il	**ricercatore**	researcher
il	**riciclaggio**	recycling
il	**riscaldamento globale**	global warming
gli	**scienziati**	scientists
lo	**strato di ozono**	ozone layer
lo	**sviluppo sostenibile**	sustainable development
l'	**universo**	universe

USEFUL PHRASES

ha molto rispetto per l'ambiente he's/she's very environmentally-minded

un prodotto ecologico an eco-friendly product

in futuro in the future

distruggere to destroy

inquinare to pollute; contaminare to contaminate

vietare to ban

salvare to save

riciclare to recycle

verde green

USEFUL WORDS *(feminine)*

le	**acque di scolo**	sewage
la	**bomboletta**	aerosol
la	**catastrofe**	disaster
la	**chiazza di petrolio**	oil slick
la	**contaminazione**	contamination
la	**discarica** *(pl -che)*	dumping ground
l'	**energia eolica**	wind power
l'	**energia nucleare**	nuclear power
l'	**energia rinnovabile**	renewable energy
la	**foresta pluviale**	rainforest
la	**luna**	moon
la	**marmitta catalitica**	catalytic converter
la	**pioggia acida**	acid rain
la	**popolazione**	population
la	**raccolta differenziata (dei rifiuti)**	separate collection of household waste
le	**scorie nucleari/ industriali**	nuclear/industrial waste

USEFUL PHRASES

biodegradabile **biodegradable**
dannoso(a) per l'ambiente **harmful to the environment**
biologico(a) **organic; biological**
ecologico(a) **environment-friendly**
benzina senza piombo **unleaded petrol**
le specie in via di estinzione **endangered species**

ESSENTIAL WORDS *(masculine)*

gli	**adulti**	adults
il	**bambino**	child; baby; little boy
il	**cognome**	surname
il	**cognome da ragazza**	maiden name
il	**cugino**	cousin
l'	**età** *(pl inv)*	age
il	**fidanzato**	fiancé
il	**figlio**	son
il	**fratello**	brother
i	**genitori**	parents
il	**giovane**	youth, young man
i	**giovani**	young people
i	**grandi**	grown-ups
il	**marito**	husband
il	**nome**	name
il	**nome (di battesimo)**	first or Christian name
i	**nonni**	grandparents
il	**nonno**	grandfather
il	**padre**	father
il	**papà** *(pl inv)*	daddy
il	**parente**	relative
il	**ragazzo**	boy; boyfriend
un	**uomo** *(pl uomini)*	man
lo	**zio** *(pl zii)*	uncle

USEFUL PHRASES

quanti anni hai (*or* ha)? **how old are you?**
ho 15 anni – ha 40 anni **I'm 15 – he/she is 40**
come ti chiami (*or* si chiama)? **what is your name?**
mi chiamo Daniela **my name is Daniela**
si chiama Paolo **his name is Paolo**
fidanzato(a) **engaged**; sposato(a) **married**
divorziato(a) **divorced**; separato(a) **separated**
sposarsi con qn **to marry sb**
sposarsi **to get married**; divorziare **to get divorced**

ESSENTIAL WORDS *(feminine)*

la	**bambina**	child; baby girl; little girl
la	**cugina**	cousin
la	**donna**	woman
la	**famiglia**	family
la	**fidanzata**	fiancée
la	**figlia**	daughter
la	**gente**	people
la	**gioventù**	youth
la	**madre**	mother
la	**mamma**	mummy
la	**moglie**	wife
la	**nonna**	grandmother
la	**persona**	person
la	**ragazza**	girl; girlfriend
la	**signora**	lady
la	**sorella**	sister
la	**zia**	aunt

USEFUL PHRASES

più giovane/vecchio(a) di me younger/older than me
hai (*or* ha) fratelli o sorelle? do you have any brothers or sisters?
ho un fratello e una sorella I have one brother and one sister
non ho fratelli I don't have any brothers or sisters
sono figlio(a) unico(a) I am an only child
tutta la famiglia the whole family
crescere to grow
invecchiare, diventare vecchio(a) to get old
vado d'accordo con i miei genitori I get on well with my parents
mia madre lavora my mother works

IMPORTANT WORDS (*masculine*)

un	**adolescente**	teenager
un	**assegno familiare**	child benefit
il	**bimbo**	child; baby; little boy
il	**neonato**	newborn baby
i	**nipoti**	grandchildren; nieces and nephews
il	**nipote**	grandson; nephew
il	**patrigno**	stepfather
lo	**scapolo**	bachelor
il	**single** (*pl inv*)	single man
il	**suocero**	father-in-law
il	**vedovo**	widower
il	**vicino**	neighbour

USEFUL WORDS (*masculine*)

il	**cognato**	brother-in-law
il	**figliastro**	stepson
il	**figlioccio**	godson
il	**fratellastro**	stepbrother
i	**gemelli**	twins
il	**genero**	son-in-law
un	**orfano**	orphan
il	**padrino**	godfather
il	**pensionato**	pensioner
il	**soprannome**	nickname
gli	**sposi novelli**	newlyweds
lo	**sposo**	bridegroom
un	**uomo anziano** (*pl uomini -i*)	old man
il	**vecchio**	old man

USEFUL PHRASES

nascere to be born; vivere to live; morire to die
sono nato nel 1990 I was born in 1990
mia nonna è morta my grandmother is dead
è morta nel 1995 she died in 1995

IMPORTANT WORDS *(feminine)*

un'	**adolescente**	teenager
la	**bimba**	child; baby girl; little girl
la	**matrigna**	stepmother
la	**neonata**	newborn baby
la	**nipote**	granddaughter; niece
la	**ragazza alla pari**	au pair girl
la	**ragazza madre**	single mother
la	**single** *(pl inv)*	single woman
la	**suocera**	mother-in-law
la	**vedova**	widow
la	**vicina**	neighbour

USEFUL WORDS *(feminine)*

la	**baby sitter** *(pl inv)*	baby sitter; nanny
la	**casalinga** *(pl -ghe)*	housewife
la	**cognata**	sister-in-law
la	**coppia**	couple
la	**donna anziana**	old woman
la	**figliastra**	stepdaughter
la	**figlioccia** *(pl -ce)*	goddaughter
le	**gemelle**	twins
la	**madrina**	godmother
la	**nuora**	daughter-in-law
un'	**orfana**	orphan
la	**pensionata**	pensioner
la	**persona anziana**	old person
la	**sorellastra**	stepsister
la	**sposa**	bride
la	**vecchia**	old woman
la	**vecchiaia**	old age

USEFUL PHRASES

è single he/she is single
è vedovo he is a widower; è vedova she is a widow
sono la più giovane I am the youngest; sono la più vecchia I am the eldest
la mia sorella maggiore my older sister
adottare un bambino to adopt a child
prendere un bambino in affidamento to foster a child

ESSENTIAL WORDS *(masculine)*

un	**agricoltore**	farmer *(cultivating crops)*
un	**allevatore**	farmer *(raising animals)*
un	**animale**	animal
il	**bosco** *(pl -chi)*	woods; forest
il	**bue** *(pl buoi)*	ox
il	**campo**	field
il	**cancello**	gate
il	**cane**	dog
il	**cane pastore**	sheepdog
il	**capretto**	kid
il	**cavallo**	horse
il	**contadino**	farmer *(cultivating crops)*
il	**furgone**	van
il	**gatto**	cat
il	**maiale**	pig
il	**paese**	village
il	**pollo**	chicken
il	**tacchino**	turkey
il	**vitello**	calf

IMPORTANT WORDS *(masculine)*

un	**agnello**	lamb
il	**fattore**	farmer
il	**gallo**	cock
il	**trattore**	tractor

USEFUL PHRASES

un campo di grano a cornfield
l'agricoltura biologica organic farming
polli ruspanti free range chickens
uova di galline da cortile free range eggs
badare agli animali to look after the animals
raccogliere to harvest
raccogliere frutta/il grano to harvest fruit/grain

ESSENTIAL WORDS *(feminine)*

un'	anatra	duck
la	campagna	country
la	cavalla	mare
la	contadina	farmer *(crops)*
la	fattoria	farm; farmhouse
la	gallina	hen
la	mucca *(pl -che)*	cow
la	pecora	sheep; ewe
la	scrofa	sow
la	serra	greenhouse
la	terra	ground; soil; earth
la	vacca *(pl -che)*	cow

IMPORTANT WORDS *(feminine)*

la	collina	hill
la	forca *(pl -che)*	fork
la	vanga *(pl -ghe)*	spade
la	zappa	hoe

USEFUL PHRASES

vivere in campagna to live in the country
lavorare in una fattoria to work on a farm
raccogliere il fieno to make hay

USEFUL WORDS *(masculine)*

un	allevamento	farm *(with livestock)*
un	aratro	plough
un	ariete	ram
un	asino	donkey
il	bestiame	cattle
il	capanno	shed
il	carro	cart
il	cereale	cereal
il	concime	manure; fertilizer
il	covone	haystack
il	fango	mud
il	fertilizzante	fertilizer
il	fienile	hayloft
il	fieno	hay
il	fossato	ditch
il	granaio	barn
il	grano	corn; wheat
il	gregge	flock *(sheep)*
il	letame	manure
il	mais	maize
il	mercato	market
il	montone	ram
il	mulino (a vento)	(wind)mill
l'	orzo	barley
il	paesaggio	landscape
il	pastore	shepherd
il	pollaio	henhouse
il	porcile	pigsty
il	pulcino	chick
il	puledro	foal
il	raccolto	crop; harvest
il	seme	seed
il	solco *(pl -chi)*	furrow
lo	spaventapasseri *(pl inv)*	scarecrow
lo	stagno	pond
il	suolo	ground, soil
il	toro	bull
il	vino	vine

USEFUL WORDS *(feminine)*

un'	**aia**	farmyard
l'	**avena**	oats
la	**brughiera**	moor, heath
la	**capra**	goat
la	**capretta**	kid
la	**falce**	sickle
la	**lana**	wool
la	**mandria**	herd *(cattle)*
la	**mietitrebbia**	combine harvester
un'	**oca** *(pl -che)*	goose
la	**paglia**	straw
la	**scala**	ladder
la	**segale**	rye
la	**stalla**	cow shed; stable
l'	**uva**	grapes
la	**vendemmia**	grape harvest, grape picking

USEFUL PHRASES

coltivare to grow *(crops etc)*
mungere una vacca to milk a cow
macellare to slaughter *(animal)*

ESSENTIAL WORDS (*masculine*)

i	frutti di mare	seafood
il	pesce	fish
il	pesce rosso	goldfish

IMPORTANT WORDS (*masculine*)

il	granchio	crab
un	insetto	insect

USEFUL WORDS (*masculine*)

un	acquario	aquarium
il	baco da seta	silkworm
il	bruco (*pl* -chi)	caterpillar
il	calabrone	hornet
il	calamaro	squid
un	eglefino	haddock
il	gambero	shrimp
il	gambero d'acqua dolce	crayfish
il	girino	tadpole
il	grillo	cricket
il	luccio	pike
il	merluzzo	cod
il	moscerino	midge
il	polpo	octopus
il	ragno	spider
il	salmone	salmon
gli	scampi	scampi
lo	scarafaggio	cockroach
lo	squalo	shark
il	tonno	tuna
il	verme	worm

USEFUL PHRASES
nuotare to swim
volare to fly
stiamo andando a pescare we're going fishing

ESSENTIAL WORDS (*feminine*)

l' **acqua**   water

IMPORTANT WORDS (*feminine*)

la **mosca** (*pl* -che)   fly
la **sardina**   sardine
la **trota**   trout

USEFUL WORDS (*feminine*)

un' **ala**   wing
un' **allergia**   allergy
un' **anguilla**   eel
un' **ape**   bee
un' **aragosta**   lobster
un' **aringa** (*pl* -ghe)   herring
la **cavalletta**   grasshopper
la **cicala**   cicada
la **cimice**   bed bug
la **coccinella**   ladybird
la **cozza**   mussel
la **falena**   moth
la **farfalla**   butterfly
la **formica** (*pl* -che)   ant
la **libellula**   dragonfly
la **medusa**   jellyfish
un' **ostrica** (*pl* -che)   oyster
la **pulce**   flea
la **rana**   frog
la **sogliola**   sole
la **tarma**   moth (*clothes*)
la **vespa**   wasp
la **zanzara**   mosquito

USEFUL PHRASES

una puntura di vespa a wasp sting
una ragnatela a spider's web

ESSENTIAL WORDS *(masculine)*

l'	aceto	vinegar
gli	antipasti	starters
un	aperitivo	aperitif
un	arrosto	roast
il	bar *(pl inv)*	café-bar
il	bicchiere	glass
il	brodo	(clear) soup, bouillon
il	burro	butter
il	caffè *(pl inv)*	coffee; café
il	caffelatte *(pl inv)*	coffee with milk
il	cameriere	waiter
i	cereali	cereal
il	cibo	food
il	cibo in scatola	tinned food
il	coltello	knife
il	conto	bill
il	croissant *(pl inv)*	croissant
il	cucchiaino	teaspoon
il	cucchiaio	spoon
il	cuoco *(pl -chi)*	cook
il	dessert *(pl inv)*	dessert
il	dolce	sweet, dessert
il	filetto	steak
il	filoncino	French stick
il	formaggio	cheese
i	frutti di mare	seafood
il	frutto *(pl f frutta)*	piece of fruit
il	gelato	ice cream
un	hamburger *(pl inv)*	hamburger
il	latte	milk
il	litro	litre
il	maiale	pork
il	menù *(pl inv)*	menu
il	menù a prezzo fisso	fixed-price menu
l'	olio	oil
il	pane	bread
il	pane tostato	toast
il	panino	bread roll; sandwich

ESSENTIAL WORDS *(feminine)*

l' acqua (minerale)	(mineral) water
la bibita	soft drink
la birra	beer
la birra alla spina	draught beer
la bistecca *(pl -che)*	steak
la bottiglia	bottle
le caramelle	sweets
la carne	meat
la carne di manzo	beef
la cena	dinner
la cioccolata (calda)	(hot) chocolate
la Coca Cola® *(pl -che -e)*	Coke®
la colazione	breakfast
la crêpe *(pl inv)*	pancake
un' entrecôte *(pl inv)*	(entrecôte) steak
la fame	hunger
la fetta	slice
la forchetta	fork
la frutta	fruit
un' insalata	salad
un' insalata mista	mixed salad
la lattina	can
la limonata	lemonade
la marmellata	jam
la marmellata d'arance	marmalade
la minestra	soup
un' oliva	olive
un' omelette *(pl inv)*	omelette
la pasta	pastry; small cake
la pasticceria	cake shop
le patatine	crisps
le patatine fritte	chips, fries
la pescheria	fish shop
la salsiccia *(pl -ce)*	sausage
la scatola	tin, can; box
la sete	thirst
le stoviglie	dishes

ESSENTIAL WORDS *(masculine continued)*

il	**pasto pronto**	ready-made meal
il	**pesce**	fish
il	**piatto**	plate; dish; course
il	**piatto del giorno**	today's special
il	**picnic** *(pl inv)*	picnic
il	**pollo (arrosto)**	(roast) chicken
il	**pranzo**	lunch
il	**primo (piatto)**	first course
il	**prosciutto**	ham
il	**prosciutto cotto**	cooked ham
il	**prosciutto crudo**	cured ham
un	**quarto**	quarter *(bottle/litre etc)*
il	**riso**	rice
il	**ristorante**	restaurant
il	**salame**	salami
il	**sale**	salt
il	**secondo (piatto)**	main course
il	**servizio**	service
il	**succo di frutta**	fruit juice
il	**tè** *(pl inv)*	tea
il	**toast** *(pl inv)*	toasted sandwich
un	**uovo** *(pl* **fuova** *)*	egg
un	**uovo alla coque**	soft-boiled egg
un	**uovo sodo**	hard-boiled egg
il	**vino**	wine
il	**vitello**	veal
lo	**yogurt** *(pl inv)*	yoghurt
lo	**zucchero**	sugar

USEFUL PHRASES

cucinare to cook; mangiare to eat
bere to drink; inghiottire to swallow
il mio piatto preferito my favourite dish
cosa vuoi da bere? what are you having to drink?
è buono it's nice
avere fame, essere affamato(a) to be hungry
avere sete, essere assetato(a) to be thirsty

ESSENTIAL WORDS *(feminine continued)*

la	tavola	table
la	tazza	cup
la	torta	cake
la	trattoria	restaurant
le	uova	eggs
le	verdure	vegetables
la	zuppa	soup

IMPORTANT WORDS *(feminine)*

la	brocca *(pl -che)*	jug
la	cameriera	waitress
la	capocuoca *(pl -che)*	chef
la	caraffa	carafe
la	carne alla griglia	grilled meat
la	carne macinata	mince
la	cotoletta di maiale	pork chop
la	crostata	tart
la	cuoca *(pl -che)*	cook
la	farina	flour
le	lumache	snails
la	maionese	mayonnaise
la	mancia *(pl -ce)*	tip
la	mensa	canteen
la	merendina	snack
la	panna	cream
la	pizza	pizza
la	ricetta	recipe
la	scelta	choice
la	scodella	bowl
la	senape	mustard
la	teiera	teapot
la	vaniglia	vanilla

IMPORTANT WORDS *(masculine)*

l'	aglio	garlic
un	agnello	lamb
il	bricco *(pl -chi)* del latte	milk jug
il	capocuoco *(pl -chi)*	chef
il	carrello	trolley
lo	chef *(pl inv)*	chef
il	coniglio	rabbit
il	coperto	cover charge; place setting
il	cordiale	cordial
il	cucchiaio da portata	tablespoon
il	digestivo	after-dinner liqueur
il	gusto	taste; flavour
il	montone	mutton
un	odore	smell
il	peperone	bell pepper
il	prezzo fisso	set price
il	prezzo tutto compreso	inclusive price
il	sapore	flavour
lo	sciroppo	syrup
lo	spuntino	snack, bite to eat
il	supplemento	extra charge
il	vitello	veal

USEFUL WORDS *(masculine)*

l'	apribottiglie *(pl inv)*	bottle opener
un	apriscatole *(pl inv)*	tin opener
il	brandy *(pl inv)*	brandy
il	cacao	cocoa
il	cavatappi *(pl inv)*	corkscrew
lo	champagne *(pl inv)*	champagne
il	cibo	food
il	cubetto di ghiaccio	ice cube
il	fegato	liver
il	ketchup *(pl inv)*	ketchup
il	miele	honey
il	panettone	cake eaten at Christmas
il	panino dolce	sweet bun

USEFUL WORDS *(feminine)*

la	briciola	crumb
la	cannuccia *(pl -ce)*	straw
la	carta dei vini	wine list
la	cotoletta	chop
le	cozze	mussels
la	crema	custard
la	fetta di pane tostato	Melba toast
la	gelatina	jelly
la	limonata	freshly-squeezed lemon juice
la	margarina	margarine
la	pancetta	bacon
la	panna montata	whipped cream
la	panna per cucina	cream for cooking
la	pasta	pasta
la	pasta in bianco	plain pasta *(with butter/oil)*
la	pasta in brodo	pasta in broth
la	pastasciutta	pasta in a sauce
la	roba da mangiare	food
la	salsa	sauce
la	selvaggina	game
la	tisana	herbal tea
la	tovaglia	tablecloth
la	trippa	tripe

USEFUL PHRASES

lavare i piatti to do the dishes
quando torniamo da scuola facciamo merenda we have a snack when we
   come back from school
fare colazione to have breakfast
delizioso(a) delicious; disgustoso(a) disgusting
buon appetito! enjoy your meal!; salute! cheers!
il conto, per favore! the bill please!
"il servizio non è compreso" "service not included"
mangiare fuori to eat out
invitare qn a pranzo to invite sb to lunch
prendere qualcosa da bere to have drinks

USEFUL WORDS (*masculine continued*)

il	**parmigiano**	parmesan cheese
il	**pasticcino**	petit four; fancy cake
il	**pasto**	meal
il	**pâté** (*pl inv*)	pâté
il	**pesto**	pesto sauce
il	**piattino**	saucer
il	**pollame**	poultry
il	**proprietario**	owner
il	**puré di patate**	mashed potatoes
il	**risotto**	risotto
il	**roastbeef** (*pl inv*)	roast beef
il	**rognone**	kidneys
il	**sandwich** (*pl inv*)	sandwich
il	**self-service** (*pl inv*)	self-service restaurant
il	**sidro**	cider
lo	**spiedino**	kebab; skewer
lo	**stufato**	stew
il	**sugo** (*pl* -ghi) **di carne**	gravy
il	**tappo**	cork
il	**thermos** (*pl inv*)	flask
il	**tovagliolo**	napkin
il	**vassoio**	tray
il	**whisky** (*pl inv*)	whisky

USEFUL PHRASES

apparecchiare la tavola to set the table
sparecchiare la tavola to clear the table
pranzare to have lunch
cenare to have dinner
assaggiare qc to taste sth
che buon profumo! that smells good!
vino bianco/rosso/rosato white/red wine/rosé
una bistecca al sangue/a media cottura/ben cotta a rare/medium/well-done steak
un toast con formaggio e prosciutto a ham and cheese toastie

SMOKING

un	accendino	lighter
il	cerino	match (*made of wax*)
il	fiammifero	match
il	fumatore	smoker
la	fumatrice	smoker
il	pacchetto di sigarette	packet of cigarettes
la	pipa	pipe
il	portacenere (*pl inv*)	ashtray
la	sigaretta	cigarette
il	sigaro	cigar
il	tabaccaio	tobacconist's
il	tabacco	tobacco

USEFUL PHRASES

una scatola di fiammiferi a box of matches
hai (*or* ha) da accendere? do you have a light?
accendere una sigaretta to light up
"vietato fumare" "no smoking"
non fumo I don't smoke
ho smesso di fumare I've stopped smoking
fumare fa molto male alla salute smoking is very bad for you

ESSENTIAL WORDS *(masculine)*

un	amico *(pl -ci)* di penna	pen friend
il	ballo	dance
il	biglietto	ticket
il	calcetto	table football
il	cantante	singer
il	canto	singing
il	CD *(pl inv)*	CD
il	cellulare	mobile phone
il	cinema *(pl inv)*	cinema
il	concerto	concert
il	decoder *(pl inv)*	digibox
il	dépliant *(pl inv)*	leaflet
il	disco *(pl -chi)*	record
il	divertimento	entertainment; pastime
il	DVD *(pl inv)*	DVD
il	film *(pl inv)*	film *(movie)*
il	fine settimana *(pl inv)*	weekend
il	fumetto	comic strip
il	gioco *(pl -chi)*	game
il	giornale	newspaper
un	hobby *(pl inv)*	hobby
	Internet	internet
un	iPod® *(pl inv)*	iPod
il	lettore CD/DVD/MP3	CD/DVD/MP3 player
il	museo	museum; art gallery
il	passatempo	hobby
il	programma	programme
il	romanzo	novel
il	romanzo giallo	detective novel
gli	scacchi	chess
lo	schermo al plasma	plasma screen
il	socio	member *(of club)*
lo	spettacolo	show
lo	sport *(pl inv)*	sport
il	teatro	theatre
il	telegiornale	TV news
il	tempo libero	free time
il	videogioco *(pl -chi)*	video game

ESSENTIAL WORDS *(feminine)*

un'	**amica** *(pl-che)***di penna**	pen friend
un'	**antenna parabolica** *(pl-e -che)*	satellite dish
la	**cantante**	singer
la	**canzone**	song
le	**carte da gioco**	cards
la	**console per videogiochi** *(pl inv)*	games console
la	**discoteca** *(pl-che)*	disco; night club
un'	**escursione**	trip; outing; hike
la	**festa**	party
la	**foto** *(pl inv)*	photo
la	**lettura**	reading
la	**macchina fotografica** *(pl-e -che)*	camera
la	**musica (pop/classica)**	(pop/classical) music
la	**paghetta**	pocket money
la	**passeggiata**	walk
la	**pellicola**	film *(for camera)*
la	**pista di pattinaggio**	skating rink
la	**pubblicità** *(pl inv)*	publicity; advert
la	**radio** *(pl inv)*	radio
la	**rivista**	magazine
la	**stampa**	the press
la	**star** *(m+f pl inv)*	film star
la	**televisione**	television
la	**TV** *(pl inv)*	TV
la	**TV satellitare**	satellite TV

USEFUL PHRASES

esco con i miei amici I go out with my friends
leggo il giornale I read the newspaper
guardo la televisione I watch television
gioco a calcio/tennis/carte I play football/tennis/cards
fare bricolage to do DIY
fare il/la baby sitter to baby-sit
fare zapping to channel-hop
andare in discoteca to go clubbing

IMPORTANT WORDS *(masculine)*

gli	annunci (sul giornale)	adverts; small ads
il	cartone animato	cartoon
il	computer *(pl inv)*	computer
il	concorso	competition
il	disegno	drawing
il	giocattolo	toy
un	incontro	meeting
un	manifesto	notice; poster
il	masterizzatore CD/DVD	CD/DVD writer
il	messaggino	text message
il	PC *(pl inv)*	PC
il	quadro	painting
il	ragazzo	boy; boyfriend
il	sito web	website
un	sms *(pl inv)*	text message

USEFUL WORDS *(masculine)*

il	blog *(pl inv)*	blog
il	campeggio	campsite; holiday camp
il	coro	choir
il	cruciverba *(pl inv)*	crossword puzzle(s)
il	fan *(pl inv)*	fan
il	gioco *(pl -chi)* da tavolo	board game
il	monopattino	scooter
il	night club *(pl inv)*	night club
i	pattini in linea	rollerblades
lo	scout *(pl inv)*	scout
lo	skateboard *(pl inv)*	skateboard

USEFUL PHRASES

emozionante **exciting**
noioso(a) **boring**
divertente **funny**
lavorare a maglia **to knit**
cucire **to sew**

IMPORTANT WORDS *(feminine)*

la **collezione**	collection
la **macchina fotografica digitale**	digital camera
la **mostra**	exhibition
la **notte**	evening; night
la **pittura**	painting
la **ragazza**	girl; girlfriend
la **sera**	evening
la **serie televisiva**	serial
la **telenovela** *(pl inv)*	soap (opera)
la **videocamera**	camcorder

USEFUL WORDS *(feminine)*

la **chat** *(pl inv)*	chat; chatroom
la **diapositiva**	slide
la **fan** *(pl inv)*	fan
la **fotografia**	photograph; photography
la **hit parade** *(pl inv)*	charts
le **parole crociate**	crossword puzzle(s)
la **scout** *(pl inv)*	girl scout

USEFUL PHRASES

non è male **it's not bad**
abbastanza bello(a) **quite good**
ballare **to dance**
fare fotografie **to take photos**
mi annoio **I'm bored**
ci vediamo di venerdì **we meet on Fridays**
sto risparmiando per comprare un lettore DVD **I'm saving up to buy a DVD recorder**
mi piacerebbe fare il giro del mondo **I'd like to go round the world**

ESSENTIAL WORDS (*masculine*)

un	**ananas** (*pl inv*)	pineapple
il	**frutto** (*pl f frutta*)	(piece of) fruit
il	**lampone**	raspberry
il	**limone**	lemon
il	**pomodoro**	tomato
il	**pompelmo**	grapefruit

IMPORTANT WORDS (*masculine*)

un	**albero da frutta**	fruit tree
il	**melone**	melon

USEFUL WORDS (*masculine*)

un	**avocado** (*pl inv*)	avocado
il	**dattero**	date
il	**fico** (*pl -chi*)	fig
il	**kiwi** (*pl inv*)	kiwi fruit
il	**mandarino**	tangerine
il	**mirtillo**	blueberry
il	**nocciolo**	stone (*in fruit*)
il	**rabarbaro**	rhubarb
il	**ribes** (*pl inv*) **nero**	blackcurrant
il	**ribes** (*pl inv*) **rosso**	redcurrant
il	**semino**	pip (*in fruit*)

USEFUL PHRASES
maturo(a) **ripe**
acerbo(a) **unripe**
un chilo di **a kilo of**
mezzo chilo di **half a kilo of**
un cestino di lamponi **a punnet of raspberries**

ESSENTIAL WORDS *(feminine)*

un'	albicocca *(pl -che)*	apricot
un'	arancia *(pl -ce)*	orange
la	banana	banana
la	buccia *(pl -ce)*	skin
la	caldarrosta	(roasted) chestnut
la	castagna	chestnut
la	ciliegia *(pl -ge)*	cherry
la	fragola	strawberry
la	frutta	fruit
la	mela	apple
la	pera	pear
la	pesca *(pl -che)*	peach
la	pescanoce	nectarine
l'	uva	grapes
l'	uvetta	raisin

USEFUL WORDS *(feminine)*

un'	arachide	peanut
la	bacca *(pl -che)*	berry
la	melagrana	pomegranate
la	mora	blackberry
la	nocciola	hazelnut
la	noce	walnut
la	noce di anacardo	cashew nut
la	noce di cocco	coconut
la	prugna	plum
la	prugna secca *(pl -e -che)*	prune
l'	uva spina	gooseberry
la	vite	vine

USEFUL PHRASES

un succo d'arancia/d'ananas an orange/a pineapple juice
un grappolo d'uva a bunch of grapes
sbucciare un frutto to peel a fruit
scivolare su una buccia di banana to slip on a banana skin

ESSENTIAL WORDS (*masculine*)

un	armadietto	cupboard
un	armadio	wardrobe
il	calorifero	radiator
il	congelatore	freezer
il	fornello (elettrico/a gas)	(electric/gas) cooker
il	frigo (*pl* -ghi)	fridge
il	frigorifero	refrigerator
il	guardaroba (*pl inv*)	wardrobe
il	letto	bed
il	mobile	piece of furniture
i	mobili	furniture
un	orologio	clock
il	paralume (*pl inv*)	lampshade
lo	scaffale	shelf
lo	specchio	mirror
il	tavolo	table
il	telefono	telephone

IMPORTANT WORDS (*masculine*)

il	baule	chest
il	bollitore	kettle
il	cellulare	mobile phone
il	divano	sofa
un	elettrodomestico	domestic appliance
il	ferro da stiro	iron
il	forno a microonde	microwave oven
il	lettore di CD/DVD	CD/DVD player
il	monolocale	studio flat
il	piano	piano
il	quadro	painting, picture
il	tavolino	coffee table
il	telefono cordless	cordless phone

ESSENTIAL WORDS *(feminine)*

la	lampada	lamp
la	lavastoviglie *(pl inv)*	dishwasher
la	lavatrice	washing machine
la	poltrona	armchair
la	radio *(pl inv)*	radio
la	radiosveglia	radio alarm
la	sedia	chair
la	stanza	room
la	stufa	heater
la	tavola	table
la	televisione	television

IMPORTANT WORDS *(feminine)*

un'	asciugatrice	tumble-dryer
un'	aspirapolvere *(pl inv)*	vacuum cleaner
la	credenza	sideboard
la	libreria	bookcase
la	radio digitale	digital radio
la	scrivania	(writing) desk

USEFUL WORDS (*masculine*)

un	**addetto ai traslochi**	removal man
un	**altoparlante**	loudspeaker
un	**asciugacapelli** (*pl inv*)	hairdryer
il	**camion dei traslochi** (*pl inv*)	removal van
il	**carrello**	trolley
il	**cassetto**	drawer
il	**cassettone**	chest of drawers
il	**comodino**	bedside table
il	**computer** (*pl inv*)	computer
il	**forno**	oven
i	**letti a castello**	bunk beds
il	**lettino**	cot
il	**letto a una piazza**	single bed
il	**letto matrimoniale**	double bed
il	**materasso**	mattress
i	**mobili**	furniture
il	**portaombrelli** (*pl inv*)	umbrella stand
lo	**sgabello**	stool
lo	**stereo compatto**	music centre
il	**tappeto**	rug
il	**telecomando**	remote control
il	**trasloco**	move
il	**tritatutto** (*pl inv*)	food processor

USEFUL PHRASES

un appartamento ammobiliato a furnished flat
accendere/spegnere la stufa to switch the heater on/off
ho rifatto il mio letto I've made my bed
sedersi to sit down
mettere qc in forno to put sth in the oven
tirare le tende to draw the curtains
chiudere le imposte to close the shutters

USEFUL WORDS *(feminine)*

un'	**antenna**	aerial
un'	**antenna parabolica** *(pl -e -che)*	satellite dish
la	**bilancia** *(pl -ce)*	scales
la	**cornice**	frame
la	**culla**	cradle
le	**imposte**	shutters
la	**lampada a stelo**	standard lamp
la	**lampada alogena**	halogen lamp
la	**macchina per cucire**	sewing machine
la	**moquette**	fitted carpet
la	**piantana**	standard lamp
la	**piastra per capelli**	hair straighteners
la	**scala a libretto**	step ladder
la	**segreteria telefonica** *(pl -e -che)*	answering machine
la	**tapparella**	blind
la	**tavola da stiro**	ironing board
la	**toilette**	toilet; dressing table
la	**TV a schermo panoramico**	widescreen TV
la	**videocamera**	camcorder

USEFUL PHRASES

è un appartamento di 4 stanze it's a 4-roomed flat
la colazione/la cena è pronta! breakfast/dinner is ready!
il pranzo è pronto! lunch is ready!

ESSENTIAL WORDS

le	Alpi	the Alps
gli	Appennini	Apennines
l'	Atlantico	the Atlantic
	Bruxelles	Brussels
la	Costa Azzurra	Côte d'Azur
le	Dolomiti	Dolomites
l'	est (m)	the east
l'	estero (m)	foreign countries; abroad
	Firenze	Florence
la	Germania	Germany
	Genova	Genoa
	Livorno	Leghorn
la	Lombardia	Lombardy
	Londra	London
	Marsiglia	Marseilles
il	Mediterraneo	the Mediterranean
il	Meridione	the South
	Milano	Milan
la	montagna	mountain
il	Monte Bianco	Mont Blanc
	Napoli	Naples
il	nord	the north
l'	ovest (m)	the west
	Parigi	Paris
il	passo	pass (mountain)
il	Piemonte	Piedmont
	Roma	Rome
la	Sardegna	Sardinia
la	Sicilia	Sicily
il	sud	the south
il	Tevere	the Tiber
	Torino	Turin
la	Toscana	Tuscany
il	Vaticano	the Vatican
	Venezia	Venice

IMPORTANT WORDS

Edimburgo *(f)*	Edinburgh
il Tamigi	the Thames

USEFUL WORDS

Atene	Athens
Berlino	Berlin
il canale della Manica, la Manica	English Channel
la capitale	capital
l' Estremo Oriente	the Far East
Ginevra	Geneva
le isole britanniche	the British Isles
L'Aia	The Hague
Lisbona	Lisbon
il Medio Oriente	the Middle East
Mosca	Moscow
il Pacifico	Pacific
Pechino	Beijing
il Polo Nord/Sud	the North/South Pole
la provincia *(pl* -ce)	province
Varsavia	Warsaw

USEFUL PHRASES

andare a Londra/Roma **to go to London/Rome**
andare in Lombardia **to go to Lombardy**
vengo da Milano/dal sud **I come from Milan/from the south**
all'estero **abroad**

a nord **in** *or* **to the north**
a sud **in** *or* **to the south**
a est **in** *or* **to the east**
a ovest **in** *or* **to the west**

l'Italia del sud *or* meridionale **southern Italy**
l'Italia del nord *or* settentrionale **northern Italy**

GREETINGS

ciao hello, hi; bye
come stai (*or* sta)? how are you?
come va? how are you?
bene fine (*in reply*)
piacere (di conoscerla) pleased to meet you
pronto hello (*on telephone*)
buonasera good afternoon; good evening
buonanotte good night
arrivederci goodbye
ci vediamo domani see you tomorrow
ci vediamo più tardi see you later

BEST WISHES

buon compleanno happy birthday
buon Natale merry Christmas
felice anno nuovo *or* buon anno happy New Year
buona Pasqua happy Easter
saluti best wishes
auguri best wishes
benvenuto(a) welcome
congratulazioni congratulations
buon appetito enjoy your meal
cari saluti all the best
divertiti (*or* si diverta) enjoy yourself
buona fortuna good luck
buon viaggio safe journey
salute bless you (*after a sneeze*); cheers
alla tua (*or* alla vostra, *etc*)! your health!

SURPRISE

mio Dio my goodness
cosa? what?
come? what?
capisco oh, I see
ma dai! really?
beh... well...
veramente? really?
stai scherzando? are you kidding?
che fortuna! how lucky!

POLITENESS

scusa (*or* mi scusi) I'm sorry; excuse me
per favore please
grazie thank you
no, grazie no thank you
sì, grazie yes please
di niente not at all, don't mention it, you're welcome
volentieri gladly

AGREEMENT

sì yes
naturalmente of course
d'accordo OK
va bene fine

DISAGREEMENT

no no
certo che no of course not
non esiste no way
per niente not at all
al contrario on the contrary
questa poi! well I never
che faccia tosta what a cheek
bada agli affari tuoi mind your own business

DIFFICULTIES

aiuto! help!
al fuoco! fire!
ahi! ouch!
scusa (or scusi) (I'm) sorry, excuse me, I beg your pardon
mi dispiace I'm sorry
che peccato what a pity
che seccatura what a nuisance
che noia how boring
sono stufo(a) I'm fed up
non lo sopporto più I can't stand it any more
mamma mia oh dear
è terribile how awful

ORDERS

attento(a) be careful
fermati (or si fermi) stop
ehi, tu hey, you there
fuori di qui clear off
silenzio shh
basta that's enough
vietato fumare no smoking
andiamo let's go
continua go ahead, go on

OTHERS

non ne ho idea no idea
forse perhaps, maybe
non so I don't know
posso aiutarti (or aiutarla)? can I help you?
eccoti qua there you are
ecco tieni (or tenga) here you are; take this
arrivo just coming
non preoccuparti don't worry
non ne vale la pena it's not worth it
a proposito by the way
caro(a) darling
poverino(a) poor thing
tanto meglio so much the better
non importa I don't mind; it doesn't matter
per me è lo stesso (or è uguale) it's all the same to me
che sfortuna too bad; bad luck!
dipende it depends
cosa devo fare? what shall I do?
a che scopo? what's the point?
mi dà fastidio it annoys me
mi dà ai nervi it gets on my nerves

ESSENTIAL WORDS *(masculine)*

un	**appuntamento**	appointment
il	**dentista**	dentist
il	**dottore**	doctor
un	**incidente**	accident
un	**infermiere**	(male) nurse
il	**letto**	bed
il	**medico**	doctor
un	**ospedale**	hospital
il	**paziente**	patient
lo	**stomaco**	stomach

IMPORTANT WORDS *(masculine)*

un	**antisettico**	antiseptic
il	**caldo**	heat
il	**cerotto**	(sticking) plaster
il	**cotone idrofilo**	cotton wool
il	**cucchiaio**	spoon; spoonful
il	**dolore**	pain
il	**farmacista**	chemist
il	**farmaco**	medicine, drug
il	**freddo**	cold
il	**gesso**	plaster cast
un	**intervento chirurgico**	operation, surgery
il	**Pronto Soccorso**	Accident and Emergency, A&E
il	**sangue**	blood
lo	**sciroppo**	syrup
lo	**studio medico**	surgery
un	**unguento**	ointment

USEFUL PHRASES

c'è stato un incidente there's been an accident
essere ricoverato(a) in ospedale to be admitted to hospital
devi (or deve) stare a letto you must stay in bed
essere malato(a) to be ill; sentirsi meglio to feel better
mi sono fatto male I have hurt myself
mi sono tagliato un dito I have cut my finger
mi sono slogato la caviglia I have sprained my ankle
si è rotto un braccio he has broken his arm

ESSENTIAL WORDS *(feminine)*

un'	aspirina	aspirin
la	dentista	dentist
la	dottoressa	doctor
la	farmacia	chemist's *(shop)*
la	farmacista	chemist, pharmacy
la	febbre	temperature
un'	infermiera	nurse
la	pasticca *(pl -che)*	tablet, pill
la	pastiglia	tablet, pill
la	paziente	patient
la	pillola	pill
la	salute	health

IMPORTANT WORDS *(feminine)*

un'	ambulanza	ambulance
un'	assicurazione	insurance
la	barella	stretcher
la	clinica *(pl -che)*	clinic
la	compressa	tablet
la	diarrea	diarrhoea
la	fascia *(pl -sce)*	bandage
la	ferita	wound
un'	influenza	flu
un'	ingessatura	plaster cast
un'	iniezione	injection
un'	insolazione	sunstroke
la	malattia	illness
la	medicina	medicine
un'	operazione	operation
la	ricetta	prescription
la	scottatura	burn; scald

USEFUL PHRASES

mi sono ustionato I have burnt myself
mi fa male la gola/la testa/lo stomaco I've got a sore throat/
   a headache/a stomach ache
avere la febbre to have a temperature

USEFUL WORDS *(masculine)*

un	ascesso	abscess
un	attacco *(pl -chi)*	fit
un	attacco cardiaco *(pl -chi -ci)*	heart attack
i	batteri	germs, bacteria
il	cancro	cancer
il	capogiro	dizziness
il	graffio	scratch
il	livido	bruise
il	mal di gola	sore throat
il	microbo	germ
il	morbillo	measles
il	nervo	nerve
gli	orecchioni	mumps
il	polso	pulse
il	preservativo	condom
il	ricostituente	tonic
il	riposo	rest
lo	shock *(pl inv)*	shock
lo	stress *(pl inv)*	stress
lo	svenimento	fainting
il	vaiolo	smallpox
il	veleno	poison

USEFUL PHRASES

ho sonno I'm sleepy
ho la nausea I feel sick
dimagrire to lose weight
ingrassare to put on weight
inghiottire to swallow
sanguinare to bleed
vomitare to vomit
essere in forma to be in good shape
riposare to rest

USEFUL WORDS *(feminine)*

l'	appendicite	appendicitis
l'	AIDS	AIDS
l'	articolazione	joint
la	ASL (Azienda Sanitaria Locale)	local heath centre
la	cassetta del pronto soccorso	first aid kit
la	cicatrice	scar
la	dentiera	false teeth
la	dieta	diet
un'	emicrania	migraine
un'	epidemia	epidemic
la	fasciatura	dressing
la	febbre da fieno	hay fever
la	gravidanza	pregnancy
la	guarigione	recovery
un'	infiammazione	inflammation
la	nausea	nausea
la	pomata	ointment
la	radiografia	X-ray
la	rosolia	German measles
la	scheggia *(pl -ge)*	splinter
la	sedia a rotelle	wheelchair
la	stampella	crutch
la	tonsillite	tonsillitis
la	tosse	cough
la	tosse canina	whooping cough
la	trasfusione (di sangue)	blood transfusion
la	varicella	chickenpox

USEFUL PHRASES

curare **to cure; to treat;** stare meglio **to get better**
gravemente ferito(a) **seriously injured**
sei *(or* è) assicurato(a)? **are you insured?**
sono raffreddato(a) **I have a cold**
mi fa male! **that hurts!; it hurts!**
respirare **to breathe;** svenire **to faint;** tossire **to cough**
morire **to die**
perdere conoscenza **to lose consciousness**
avere il braccio al collo **to have one's arm in a sling**

ESSENTIAL WORDS *(masculine)*

un	**albergo** *(pl -ghi)*	hotel
un	**ascensore**	lift
un	**assegno**	cheque
i	**bagagli**	luggage
il	**bagno**	bathroom
il	**balcone**	balcony
il	**bar** *(pl inv)*	bar
il	**cameriere**	waiter
il	**conto**	bill
il	**direttore**	manager
il	**facchino**	porter
un	**hotel** *(pl inv)*	hotel
i	**letti gemelli**	twin beds
il	**letto matrimoniale**	double bed
il	**modulo**	form
il	**numero**	number
un	**ospite**	guest
il	**passaporto**	passport
il	**pasto**	lunch; meal
il	**piano**	floor; storey
il	**pianoterra**	ground floor
il	**pranzo**	lunch
il	**prezzo**	price
un	**receptionist** *(pl inv)*	receptionist
il	**ristorante**	restaurant
il	**rumore**	noise
il	**soggiorno**	stay
gli	**spiccioli**	change, loose coins
il	**telefono**	telephone

USEFUL PHRASES

vorrei prenotare una camera I would like to book a room
una camera con doccia/bagno a room with a shower/bathroom
una camera singola/matrimoniale a single/double room
una camera a due letti a twin-bedded room

ESSENTIAL WORDS *(feminine)*

la **camera**	room
la **cameriera**	waitress; chambermaid
la **caparra**	deposit
la **carta di credito**	credit card
la **chiave**	key
la **colazione**	breakfast
la **comodità** *(pl inv)*	comfort; convenience
la **data**	date
la **direttrice**	manager
la **doccia** *(pl -ce)*	shower
la **mezza pensione**	half board
la **notte**	night
un' **ospite**	guest
la **pensione**	guest house
la **pensione completa**	full board
la **piscina**	swimming pool
la **reception** *(pl inv)*	reception
la **receptionist** *(pl inv)*	receptionist
la **scala**	ladder; staircase
la **tariffa**	rate, rates
la **televisione**	television
la **valigia** *(pl -ge)*	suitcase
la **vista**	view
le **toilette**	toilets
un' **uscita d'emergenza**	fire escape

USEFUL PHRASES

ha un documento di identità? do you have any ID?
a che ora è servita la colazione? what time is breakfast served?
pulire la stanza to clean the room
"non disturbare" "do not disturb"

IMPORTANT WORDS (*masculine*)

un	**asciugamano**	towel
il	**bagno**	bathroom
il	**benvenuto**	welcome
un	**interruttore**	switch
il	**lavandino**	washbasin
il	**prezzo tutto compreso**	all inclusive price
il	**reclamo**	complaint
il	**rumore**	noise

USEFUL WORDS (*masculine*)

l'	**atrio**	foyer
il	**capocameriere**	head waiter
il	**cuoco** (*pl* -chi)	cook
il	**cuscino**	pillow
il	**rubinetto**	tap
il	**sommellier** (*pl inv*)	wine waiter

USEFUL PHRASES

occupato(a) occupied
libero(a) vacant
pulito(a) clean
sporco(a) dirty
dormire to sleep
svegliarsi to wake up
"con tutte le comodità" "with all facilities"
potrei avere la sveglia domani mattina alle sette, per favore? I'd like a 7
   o'clock alarm call tomorrow morning, please
una camera con vista sul mare a room overlooking the sea

IMPORTANT WORDS *(feminine)*

l'	acqua calda	hot water
la	fattura	bill; invoice
la	guida turistica *(pl -e -che)*	guidebook
la	mancia *(pl -ce)*	tip
la	ricevuta	receipt
la	saponetta	bar of soap
la	vasca *(pl -che)* da bagno	bathtub

USEFUL WORDS *(feminine)*

la	cassaforte *(pl casseforti)*	safe
la	carta igienica	toilet paper
la	coperta	blanket
la	corrente d'aria	draught
la	cuoca *(pl -che)*	cook

USEFUL PHRASES

una camera con mezza pensione room with half board
ci sediamo fuori? shall we sit outside?
abbiamo cenato all'aperto we were served dinner outside
un albergo a tre stelle a three-star hotel
IVA inclusa inclusive of VAT

ESSENTIAL WORDS *(masculine)*

un	(appezzamento di) terreno	plot of land
un	appartamento	flat, apartment
un	ascensore	lift
il	bagno	bathroom
il	balcone	balcony
il	box *(pl inv)*	garage
il	cancello	gate
il	condominio	block of flats
il	cortile	(court)yard
un	edificio	building
l'	esterno	exterior
il	garage *(pl inv)*	garage
il	giardino	garden
un	indirizzo	address
l'	interno	interior
il	mobile	piece of furniture
i	mobili	furniture
il	numero di telefono	phone number
il	paese	village
il	parcheggio	car park; parking space
il	piano	floor, storey; piano
il	pianoterra	ground floor
il	pianterreno	ground floor
il	quartiere residenziale	housing estate
il	riscaldamento (centralizzato)	(central) heating
il	seminterrato	basement
il	soggiorno	living room
il	viale	avenue
il	vialetto d'accesso	drive

USEFUL PHRASES

quando vado a casa when I go home
guardare fuori dalla finestra to look out of the window
a casa mia/tua/nostra at my/your/our house
traslocare to move house
affittare un appartamento to rent a flat

ESSENTIAL WORDS *(feminine)*

la	camera da letto	bedroom
la	cantina	cellar
la	casa	house
la	chiave	key
la	città *(pl inv)*	town; city
la	cucina	kitchen
la	doccia *(pl -ce)*	shower
un'	entrata	entrance
la	finestra	window
la	parete	wall
la	porta	door
la	porta d'ingresso	front door
la	sala da pranzo	dining room
le	scale	stairs
la	stanza	room
la	via	street
la	vista	view

USEFUL PHRASES

vivo in una casa/un appartamento I live in a house/flat
(al piano) di sopra upstairs
(al piano) di sotto downstairs
al primo piano on the first floor
al pianoterra on the ground floor
in casa at home

IMPORTANT WORDS (*masculine*)

l'	affitto	rent
l'	alloggio	accommodation
un	appartamento ammobiliato	furnished flat
il	bilocale	two-roomed flat
il	caminetto	fireplace
il	camino	chimney
il	corridoio	corridor
il	gabinetto	lavatory
il	lavandino	washbasin
il	mobilio	furniture
il	monolocale	studio flat
il	padrone di casa	landlord; owner
il	pianerottolo	landing
il	portinaio	caretaker; concierge
il	prato	lawn
il	proprietario	owner; landlord
il	solaio	attic
il	tetto	roof
il	trasloco (*pl*-chi)	move
il	vicino (di casa)	neighbour

USEFUL WORDS (*masculine*)

un	attico	penthouse; loft apartment
il	campanello	door bell
l'	ingresso	hall; entrance
un	inquilino	tenant; lodger
il	lucernario	skylight
il	muro	wall
il	parquet (*pl inv*)	parquet floor
il	pavimento	floor
lo	scaldabagno (elettrico)	(electric) water heater
lo	scalino	step
il	soffitto	ceiling
lo	studio	study
il	tubo	pipe
il	vetro	window pane

IMPORTANT WORDS *(feminine)*

la casetta di campagna	cottage
la donna delle pulizie	cleaner
la legnaia	lumber room
la manutenzione	upkeep; maintenance
la padrona di casa	landlady; owner
la portinaia	caretaker; concierge
la proprietaria	owner; landlady
la vicina (di casa)	neighbour

USEFUL WORDS *(feminine)*

un' antenna	aerial
la caldaia	boiler
la camera degli ospiti	spare room
la casa popolare	council flat *or* house
la casalinga *(pl -ghe)*	housewife
la decorazione	decoration
la facciata	front *(of house)*
un' imposta	shutter
un' inquilina	tenant; lodger
la mattonella	tile
la persiana	blind; shutter
la piastrella	tile
la portafinestra	French window
la portineria	caretaker's room
la siepe	hedge
la soffitta	attic
la soglia	doorstep
la tegola	roof tile; slate
la tubatura	pipe
la villetta	detached house
le villette a schiera	terraced houses

USEFUL PHRASES

bussare alla porta **to knock at the door**
ha suonato il campanello **the doorbell's just gone**
dall'esterno **from the outside**
dentro **on the inside**
fino al tetto **up to the ceiling**

ESSENTIAL WORDS (*masculine*)

un **armadietto**	cupboard
un **armadio**	wardrobe
un **asciugacapelli** (*pl inv*)	hair dryer
un **asciugamano**	towel
il **bidone della spazzatura**	dustbin
il **cuscino**	pillow; cushion
il **dentifricio**	toothpaste
il **forno**	oven
il **frigo** (*pl inv*)	fridge
il **frigorifero**	refrigerator
il **gas**	gas
un **interruttore**	switch
il **lavabo**	washbasin
il **lavandino**	sink
il **lenzuolo** (*pl f* lenzuola)	sheet
i **piatti**	dishes
il **portacenere** (*pl inv*)	ashtray
il **poster** (*pl inv*)	poster
il **quadro**	picture
il **radiatore**	radiator
il **rubinetto**	tap
il **sapone**	soap
lo **specchio**	mirror
lo **spremiagrumi** (*pl inv*)	juicer
lo **strofinaccio**	dishtowel, tea towel
il **tappeto**	carpet, rug
il **televisore**	television set
il **tovagliolo**	napkin
il **vassoio**	tray

USEFUL PHRASES
farsi un bagno **to have a bath**
farsi una doccia **to have a shower**
fare le pulizie **to do the housework**
mi piace cucinare **I like cooking**

ESSENTIAL WORDS *(feminine)*

l'	acqua	water
la	bilancia *(pl -ce)*	scales
la	caffettiera	coffee maker
la	casseruola	saucepan
la	cassetta delle lettere	letterbox
la	coperta	blanket
la	doccia *(pl -ce)*	shower
l'	elettricità	electricity
la	foto *(pl inv)*	photo
la	lampada	lamp
la	lavatrice	washing machine
le	lenzuola	sheets
la	luce	light
la	pentola	saucepan
la	radio *(pl inv)*	radio
la	spazzola	brush
le	stoviglie	dishes
la	sveglia	alarm clock
la	televisione	television
le	tende	curtains
la	vasca *(pl -che)*	bath

USEFUL PHRASES

guardare la televisione **to watch television**
alla televisione **on television**
accendere/spegnere la TV **to switch on/off the TV**
gettare qualcosa nel bidone della spazzatura **to throw sth in the dustbin**
lavare i piatti **to do the dishes**

IMPORTANT WORDS *(masculine)*

un	**aspirapolvere** *(pl inv)*	vacuum cleaner
il	**bidé** *(pl inv)*	bidet
il	**bucato**	(clean) washing
il	**calorifero**	radiator
il	**detersivo (in polvere)**	washing powder
il	**detersivo per piatti**	washing-up liquid
il	**fornello**	stove
il	**termosifone**	heater
il	**ventilatore**	electric fan

USEFUL WORDS *(masculine)*

il	**cestino**	wastepaper basket
il	**coperchio**	lid
il	**ferro da stiro**	iron
il	**forno a microonde**	microwave oven
il	**frullatore**	blender
il	**guanciale**	pillow
il	**macinacaffè** *(pl inv)*	coffee grinder
il	**mestolo**	ladle
il	**piumone**	duvet
il	**secchio**	bucket
il	**soprammobile**	ornament
lo	**straccio per la polvere**	duster
lo	**strofinaccio**	dishcloth
il	**tostapane** *(pl inv)*	toaster
il	**vaso**	vase

USEFUL PHRASES

collegare/scollegare un elettrodomestico **to plug in/to unplug an appliance**
passare l'aspirapolvere **to hoover**
fare il bucato **to do the washing**

IMPORTANT WORDS *(feminine)*

la donna delle pulizie	cleaner
la lampadina	light bulb
la lavastoviglie *(pl inv)*	dishwasher
la padella	frying pan
la piastra	hob
la pittura	paint; painting
la polvere	dust
la presa (di corrente)	socket
la prolunga *(pl -ghe)*	extension
la ricetta	recipe
la roba sporca	(dirty) washing, laundry
la serratura	lock
la spina elettrica	plug *(electric)*
la stufa	heater

USEFUL WORDS *(feminine)*

la carta da parati	wallpaper
la cera	floor polish
la coperta elettrica *(pl -e -che)*	electric blanket
la gruccia *(pl -ce)*	coat hanger
le immondizie	rubbish
la maniglia	door handle
la moquette *(pl inv)*	fitted carpet
la pentola a pressione	pressure cooker
la ringhiera	bannister
la scala	ladder; staircase
la scopa	broom
la spugna	sponge
la tappezzeria	upholstery
la tavola da stiro	ironing board

USEFUL PHRASES

scopare to sweep (up)
pulire to clean
mettere via le cose to tidy away things
lasciare in giro i giocattoli to leave toys lying about

ESSENTIAL WORDS *(masculine)*

un	acconto	deposit
un	assegno	cheque
il	Bancomat® *(pl inv)*	debit card; cash dispenser, ATM
il	cambio	exchange
il	centesimo (di euro)	euro cent
il	codice postale	postcode
il	contratto telefonico	phone contract
il	documento (di identificazione)	ID card
un	errore	mistake
un	euro *(pl inv)*	euro
il	fax *(pl inv)*	fax; fax machine
il	francobollo	postage stamp
un	impiegato (allo sportello)	counter clerk
un	indirizzo	address
il	modulo	form
il	numero	number
il	pacchetto	parcel
il	passaporto	passport
il	postino	postman
il	prefisso telefonico	dialling code
il	prezzo	price
il	segnale di libero	dialling tone
un	sms *(pl inv)*	text message
lo	sportello	counter
gli	spiccioli	small change
il	telefono	telephone
un	ufficio informazioni turistiche	tourist information office
un	ufficio postale	post office

USEFUL PHRASES

la banca più vicina the nearest bank

vorrei incassare un assegno/cambiare del denaro I would like to cash a
   cheque/to change some money

ESSENTIAL WORDS *(feminine)*

la	banca *(pl -che)*	bank
la	banconota	banknote
la	biro *(pl inv)*	Biro®
la	buca *(pl -che)* delle lettere	postbox
la	busta	envelope
la	carta di credito	credit card
la	carta di debito	debit card
la	carta d'identità	ID card
la	cartolina	postcard
la	cassa	check-out
la	chiamata	call
la	compagnia telefonica *(pl -e -che)*	phone company
la	firma	signature
un'	impiegata (allo sportello)	counter clerk
le	informazioni	information
la	lettera	letter
la	penna	pen
la	posta elettronica	email *(service)*
la	postina	postwoman
la	risposta	reply
la	sterlina	pound (sterling)

USEFUL PHRASES

una chiamata telefonica a phone call
telefonare a qn to phone sb
alzare la cornetta to lift the receiver
comporre il numero to dial (the number)
pronto – sono il signor Rossi hello, this is Mr Rossi
la linea è occupata the line is engaged
attenda in linea hold the line
ho sbagliato numero I got the wrong number
riattaccare to hang up
vorrei fare una chiamata internazionale I'd like to make an international
  phone call

IMPORTANT WORDS *(masculine)*

l'	**ADSL**	broadband
il	**cellulare**	mobile (phone)
il	**conto (in banca)**	(bank) account
il	**credito**	credit
il	**domicilio**	home address
il	**gettone**	token
un	**internet caffè** *(pl inv)*	internet café
il	**libretto degli assegni**	cheque book
il	**messaggio di posta elettronica**	email
il	**numero verde**	freephone
un	**operatore telefonico**	operator
il	**pagamento**	payment
il	**portafoglio**	wallet
il	**portamonete** *(pl inv)*	purse
il	**tasso di cambio**	exchange rate
il	**telefono fisso**	landline
il	**traveller's cheque** *(pl inv)*	traveller's cheque
un	**ufficio oggetti smarriti**	lost property office

USEFUL WORDS *(masculine)*

un	**allegato**	attachment
il	**destinatario**	addressee
il	**login** *(pl inv)*	login
il	**mittente**	sender
il	**ricevente**	receiver
un	**ufficio cambio**	bureau de change
il	**vaglia** *(pl inv)* **postale**	postal order

USEFUL PHRASES

sara punto smith chiocciola anywhere punto com **sara dot smith at anywhere dot com**

www. [voo voo voo punto] **www dot**

IMPORTANT WORDS *(feminine)*

la	banda larga	broadband
la	cabina telefonica *(pl -e -che)*	phone box
la	carta da lettera	writing paper
la	chiamata telefonica *(pl -e -che)*	phone call
la	guida telefonica *(pl -e -che)*	telephone directory
un'	imposta	tax
la	levata (della posta)	collection
la	mail *(pl inv)*	email
un'	operatrice telefonica *(pl -i -che)*	operator
la	password *(pl inv)*	password
la	posta	mail
la	ricarica *(pl -che)*	top-up (card)
la	ricompensa	reward
la	scheda telefonica *(pl -e -che)*	phonecard
la	scheda telefonica prepagata	prepaid phonecard
la	segreteria telefonica	voicemail; answering machine
la	spesa extra	extra charge
le	spese	expenses
la	tassa	tax

USEFUL WORDS *(feminine)*

la	carta da regalo	wrapping paper
la	casella postale	PO box
la	chiamata internazionale	international call
la	destinataria	addressee
la	lettera raccomandata	registered letter
la	mittente	sender
la	SIM card *(pl inv)*	SIM card
la	suoneria	ringtone

USEFUL PHRASES

ho perso il portafoglio **I've lost my wallet**
riempire un modulo **to fill in a form**
in stampatello **in block letters**
fare una chiamata a carico del ricevente **to make a reverse charge call**

GENERAL SITUATIONS

qual è il tuo (*or* **suo**) **indirizzo?** what is your address?
come si scrive? how do you spell that?
puoi (*or* **può**) **cambiarmi 100 euro?** do you have change of 100 euros?
scrivere to write
rispondere to reply
firmare to sign
puoi (*or* **può**) **aiutarmi per favore?** can you help me please?
qual è la strada per la stazione? how do I get to the station?
dritto straight on
a destra to (*or* on) the right; **a sinistra** to (*or* on) the left

LETTERS

Caro Carlo Dear Carlo
Cara Anna Dear Anna
Egr. Sig. Dear Sir
Gent. Sig.ra Dear Madam
saluti best wishes
un abbraccio da love from
baci da love from
cordiali saluti kind regards
distinti saluti yours faithfully; yours sincerely
baci e abbracci love and kisses
% PTO

E-MAILS

mandare una mail a qn to email sb

MOBILES

mandare un sms a qn to text sb

PRONUNCIATION GUIDE

Pronounced approximately as:

A	ah
B	bee
C	chee
D	dee
E	ay
F	ef-fay
G	djee
H	ak-ka
I	ee
J	ee loonga
K	kap-pa
L	el-lay
M	em-may
N	en-nay
O	oh
P	pee
Q	koo
R	er-ray
S	es-say
T	tee
U	oo
V	vee
W	dop-pya voo
X	eeks
Y	eepsilon
Z	dzay-ta

ESSENTIAL WORDS *(masculine)*

un	avvocato	lawyer
i	documenti	papers
il	furto	burglary; theft
un	incendio	fire
un	incidente	accident
il	passaporto	passport
il	problema	problem

IMPORTANT WORDS *(masculine)*

un	aggressore	mugger
il	carabiniere	policeman
il	colpevole	culprit
il	commissariato (di polizia)	police station
il	consolato	consulate
il	danno *or* i danni	damage
un	esercito	army
il	governo	government
il	ladro	burglar; thief
il	morto	dead man
il	permesso	permission
il	poliziotto	policeman
il	posto di blocco	checkpoint; roadblock
il	proprietario	owner
il	rapinatore	robber
il	rapinatore a mano armata	armed robber
il	testimone	witness

USEFUL PHRASES

rubare to steal; to burgle; rapinare to rob
mi hanno rubato il portafoglio! someone has stolen my wallet!
illegale illegal; innocente innocent
non è colpa mia it's not my fault
aiuto! help!; al ladro! stop thief!
al fuoco! fire!; mani in alto! hands up!
rapinare una banca to rob a bank
mandare qn in prigione to send sb to prison; fuggire to escape
evadere to escape from prison

ESSENTIAL WORDS *(feminine)*

la	**carta d'identità**	ID card
la	**colpa**	fault
l'	**identità** *(pl inv)*	identity
la	**polizia**	police
la	**poliziotta**	policewoman
la	**verità** *(pl inv)*	truth

IMPORTANT WORDS *(feminine)*

un'	**aggressione**	mugging
la	**banda**	gang
la	**borsetta**	handbag
la	**colpevole**	culprit
la	**denuncia** *(pl -ce)*	report
l'	**imposta sul redito**	income tax
la	**ladra**	thief; burglar
la	**manifestazione**	demonstration
la	**morta**	dead woman
la	**morte**	death
la	**multa**	fine
la	**pena di morte**	death penalty
la	**polizza di assicurazione**	insurance policy
la	**proprietaria**	owner
la	**rapina**	hold-up, robbery
la	**rapinatrice**	robber
la	**ricompensa**	reward
la	**spia**	spy
le	**tasse**	taxes
la	**testimone**	witness

USEFUL PHRASES

una rapina a mano armata a hold-up
rapire un bambino to abduct a child
un gruppo di teppisti a bunch of hooligans
in prigione in prison
picchiarsi to fight; arrestare to arrest; accusare to charge
essere in custodia cautelare to be remanded in custody
accusare qn di qc to accuse sb of sth; to charge sb with sth

USEFUL WORDS *(masculine)*

un	arresto	arrest
un	assassinio	murder
il	bottino	loot
il	cadavere	corpse
il	carcere	prison
un	clandestino	illegal immigrant; stowaway
il	criminale	criminal
il	delitto	crime
il	detective *(pl inv)* privato	private detective
il	detenuto	prisoner
il	dirottamento aereo	hijacking
il	dirottatore	hijacker
il	drogato	drug addict
il	gangster *(pl inv)*	gangster
il	giudice	judge
un	imbroglione	crook
un	immigrato clandestino	illegal immigrant
un	omicida	murderer
un	omicidio	murder
un	ostaggio	hostage
il	piromane	arsonist
il	poliziotto	policeman
il	prigioniero	prisoner
il	processo	trial
il	riscatto	ransom
il	salvataggio	rescue
lo	sbirro	cop
il	sequestratore	kidnapper
il	sequestro	kidnapping
lo	spacciatore (di droga)	drugs pusher
lo	sparo	(gun) shot
il	tentativo	attempt
un	teppista	hooligan
il	terrorismo	terrorism
il	terrorista	terrorist
il	tossicodipendente	drug addict
il	trafficante di droga	drug dealer
il	tribunale	court

USEFUL WORDS *(feminine)*

l'	accusa	the prosecution; charge
un'	assassina	murderer
la	bomba	bomb
la	clandestina	illegal immigrant; stowaway
la	criminale	criminal
la	custodia cautelare	custody
la	delinquente	criminal
la	detective *(pl inv)* privata	private detective
la	detenuta	prisoner
la	detenzione	imprisonment
la	dichiarazione	statement
la	difesa	defence
la	dirottatrice	hijacker
la	droga *(pl -ghe)*	drug
la	drogata	drug addict
la	fuga *(pl -ghe)*	escape
la	giuria	jury
la	guardia	guard; warden
un'	immigrata clandestina	illegal immigrant
un'	inchiesta	inquiry
un'	insurrezione	uprising
la	legge	law
la	lite	quarrel, argument
la	multa	fine
un'	omicida	murderer
la	piromane	arsonist
la	pistola	gun
la	poliziotta	policewoman
la	prigione	prison
la	prova	proof; evidence
la	retata	raid
la	rivolta	uprising
la	sequestratrice	kidnapper
la	spacciatrice (di droga)	drugs pusher
la	teppista	hooligan
la	terrorista	terrorist
la	tossicodipendente	drug addict
la	trafficante di droga	drug dealer

ESSENTIAL WORDS (masculine)

l'	acciaio	steel
l'	argento	silver
il	cotone	cotton
il	cristallo	crystal
il	cuoio	leather
il	ferro	iron
il	gas	gas
il	gasolio	diesel
il	legno	wood
il	metallo	metal
l'	oro	gold
il	vetro	glass

IMPORTANT WORDS (masculine)

l'	acciaio inossidabile	stainless steel
l'	alluminio	aluminium
il	cartone	cardboard
il	ferro battuto	wrought iron
il	mattone	brick
lo	stato	condition
il	tessuto	fabric

USEFUL PHRASES

una sedia di legno a wooden chair
una cassa di plastica a plastic box
un anello d'oro a gold ring
in buone condizioni in good condition
in cattive condizioni in bad condition

ESSENTIAL WORDS *(feminine)*

la	**gomma**	rubber
la	**lana**	wool
la	**pelle**	leather
la	**pietra**	stone
la	**plastica**	plastic

IMPORTANT WORDS *(feminine)*

la	**carta**	paper
la	**fibra sintetica** *(pl -e -che)*	synthetic fibre
la	**seta**	silk
la	**stoffa**	fabric

USEFUL PHRASES

una pelliccia **a fur coat**
una medaglia d'oro **a gold medal**
un maglione di lana **a woollen jumper**
arrugginito(a) **rusty**

USEFUL WORDS *(masculine)*

l'	acrilico	acrylic
il	bronzo	bronze
il	carbone	coal
il	cemento	concrete
il	filo (di cotone)	thread
il	filo di ferro	wire
il	gesso	plaster
il	lino	linen
il	liquido	liquid
il	marmo	marble
il	materiale	material
l'	ottone	brass
il	piombo	lead
il	pizzo	lace
il	rame	copper
il	raso	satin
lo	stagno	tin
il	tweed	tweed
il	velluto	velvet
il	velluto a coste	corduroy
il	vimini	wickerwork

USEFUL WORDS *(feminine)*

l'	**argilla**	clay
la	**cera**	wax
la	**ceramica** *(pl -che)*	ceramics; pottery
la	**colla**	glue
la	**corda**	string
la	**creta**	clay
la	**gommapiuma**	foam rubber
la	**latta**	tinplate
la	**paglia**	straw
la	**pelle scamosciata**	suede
la	**porcellana**	china
la	**tela**	canvas

ESSENTIAL WORDS *(masculine)*

il	direttore d'orchestra	conductor
il	gruppo	band
il	musicista	musician
il	pianoforte	piano
lo	strumento musicale	musical instrument
il	violino	violin

USEFUL WORDS *(masculine)*

un	accordo	chord
un	archetto	bow
un	astuccio	case
il	basso	bass guitar
il	clarinetto	clarinet
il	contrabbasso	double bass
il	fagotto	bassoon
il	flauto	flute
il	flauto dolce	recorder
un	impianto di amplificazione	PA system
il	jazz	jazz
il	leggio *(pl -gii)*	music stand
il	microfono	microphone
il	minidisco *(pl -chi)*	minidisc
il	mixer *(pl inv)*	mixing deck
un	oboe	oboe
un	organo	organ
gli	ottoni	brass
i	piatti	cymbals
il	sassofono	saxophone
il	solista	soloist
lo	studio di registrazione	recording studio
gli	strumenti a corda	string instruments
gli	strumenti a fiato	wind instruments
gli	strumenti a percussione	percussion instruments
il	tamburello	tambourine
il	tamburo	drum
il	tasto (del piano)	(piano) key
il	trombone	trombone
il	violoncello	cello

ESSENTIAL WORDS *(feminine)*

la	**batteria**	drums, drum kit
la	**chitarra**	guitar
la	**direttrice d'orchestra**	conductor
la	**musica**	music
la	**musicista**	musician
un'	**orchestra**	orchestra

USEFUL WORDS *(feminine)*

un'	**armonica** *(pl -che)*	harmonica
un'	**arpa**	harp
la	**bacchetta**	conductor's baton
la	**banda**	brass band
la	**composizione**	composition
la	**corda**	string
la	**cornamusa**	bagpipes
la	**custodia**	case
la	**grancassa**	bass drum
la	**fisarmonica** *(pl -che)*	accordion
la	**nota**	note
la	**registrazione digitale**	digital recording
la	**solista**	soloist
la	**tromba**	trumpet; bugle
la	**viola**	viola

USEFUL PHRASES

suonare un pezzo to play a piece
suonare forte/piano to play loudly/softly
essere intonato(a)/stonato(a) to sing in tune/out of tune
suonare il piano/la chitarra to play the piano/the guitar
suonare la batteria to play drums
Paolo alla batteria Paolo on drums
esercitarsi al pianoforte to practise the piano
suoni in un gruppo? do you play in a band?
una nota falsa a wrong note

CARDINAL NUMBERS

zero	0	zero
uno (*m*), una (*f*)	1	one
due	2	two
tre	3	three
quattro	4	four
cinque	5	five
sei	6	six
sette	7	seven
otto	8	eight
nove	9	nine
dieci	10	ten
undici	11	eleven
dodici	12	twelve
tredici	13	thirteen
quattordici	14	fourteen
quindici	15	fifteen
sedici	16	sixteen
diciassette	17	seventeen
diciotto	18	eighteen
diciannove	19	nineteen
venti	20	twenty
ventuno	21	twenty-one
ventidue	22	twenty-two
ventitré	23	twenty-three
trenta	30	thirty
trentuno	31	thirty-one
trentadue	32	thirty-two
quaranta	40	forty
cinquanta	50	fifty
sessanta	60	sixty
settanta	70	seventy
ottanta	80	eighty
novanta	90	ninety
cento	100	one hundred

CARDINAL NUMBERS *(continued)*

centouno	**101**	a hundred and one
centodue	**102**	a hundred and two
centodieci	**110**	a hundred and ten
centottantadue	**182**	a hundred and eighty-two
duecento	**200**	two hundred
duecentouno	**201**	two hundred and one
duecentodue	**202**	two hundred and two
trecento	**300**	three hundred
quattrocento	**400**	four hundred
cinquecento	**500**	five hundred
seicento	**600**	six hundred
settecento	**700**	seven hundred
ottocento	**800**	eight hundred
novecento	**900**	nine hundred
mille	**1000**	one thousand
milleuno(a)	**1001**	a thousand and one
milledue	**1002**	a thousand and two
duemila	**2000**	two thousand
duemilanove	**2009**	two thousand and nine
diecimila	**10000**	ten thousand
centomila	**100000**	one hundred thousand
un milione	**1000000**	one million
due milioni	**2000000**	two million

USEFUL PHRASES

mille euro a thousand euros; duemila euro two thousand euros
un milione di dollari one million dollars
tre virgola due (3,2) three point two (3.2)

ORDINAL NUMBERS

primo(a)	$1^{\circ}, 1^{a}$	first
secondo(a)	$2^{\circ}, 2^{a}$	second
terzo(a)	$3^{\circ}, 3^{a}$	third
quarto(a)	$4^{\circ}, 4^{a}$	fourth
quinto(a)	$5^{\circ}, 5^{a}$	fifth
sesto(a)	$6^{\circ}, 6^{a}$	sixth
settimo(a)	$7^{\circ}, 7^{a}$	seventh
ottavo(a)	$8^{\circ}, 8^{a}$	eighth
nono(a)	$9^{\circ}, 9^{a}$	ninth
decimo(a)	$10^{\circ}, 10^{a}$	tenth
undicesimo(a)	$11^{\circ}, 11^{a}$	eleventh
dodicesimo(a)	$12^{\circ}, 12^{a}$	twelfth
tredicesimo(a)	$13^{\circ}, 13^{a}$	thirteenth
quattordicesimo(a)	$14^{\circ}, 14^{a}$	fourteenth
quindicesimo(a)	$15^{\circ}, 15^{a}$	fifteenth
sedicesimo(a)	$16^{\circ}, 16^{a}$	sixteenth
diciassettesimo(a)	$17^{\circ}, 17^{a}$	seventeenth
diciottesimo(a)	$18^{\circ}, 18^{a}$	eighteenth
diciannovesimo(a)	$19^{\circ}, 19^{a}$	nineteenth
ventesimo(a)	$20^{\circ}, 20^{a}$	twentieth
millesimo(a)	$1000^{\circ}, 1000^{a}$	thousandth
duemillesimo(a)	$2000^{\circ}, 2000^{a}$	two thousandth

FRACTIONS

(un) mezzo/(una) mezza	$\frac{1}{2}$	a half
uno(a) e mezzo(a)	$1\frac{1}{2}$	one and a half
due e mezzo(a)	$2\frac{1}{2}$	two and a half
un terzo	$\frac{1}{3}$	a third
due terzi	$\frac{2}{3}$	two thirds
un quarto	$\frac{1}{4}$	a quarter
tre quarti	$\frac{3}{4}$	three quarters
un sesto	$\frac{1}{6}$	a sixth
tre e cinque sesti	$3\frac{5}{6}$	three and five sixths
un settimo	$\frac{1}{7}$	a seventh
un ottavo	$\frac{1}{8}$	an eighth
un nono	$\frac{1}{9}$	a ninth
un decimo	$\frac{1}{10}$	a tenth
un undicesimo	$\frac{1}{11}$	an eleventh
un dodicesimo	$\frac{1}{12}$	a twelfth
sette dodicesimi	$\frac{7}{12}$	seven twelfths
un centesimo	$\frac{1}{100}$	a hundredth
un millesimo	$\frac{1}{1000}$	a thousandth

USEFUL PHRASES

un barattolo di a jar of; a tin or can of
un barile di a barrel of
un bicchiere di a glass of
un boccone di a mouthful of
una bottiglia di a bottle of
una cassa di a box of
centinia di hundreds of
un centinaio di (about) a hundred
un chilo di a kilo of
una cucchiaiata di a spoonful of
una decina di persone about ten people
diversi(e) several
a diversi chilometri da a few kilometres from
una dozzina di (about) a dozen
entrambi both of them
un etto di a hundred grams of
una fetta di pane a slice of bread
una fetta di prosciutto a slice of ham
una (gran) quantità di lots of
un gregge di a flock of
un gruppo di a group of
un litro di a litre of
la maggior parte di, gran parte di most (of)
una mandria di a herd of

USEFUL PHRASES

un metro di a metre of
mezza dozzina half a dozen
mezzo(a) half (of)
mezzo litro di half a litre of
migliaia di thousands of
molti(e) many; a lot of
molto(a) a lot (of); much
un mucchio di a pile of; loads of
un pacchetto di a packet of
un paio di a pair of
un pezzo di carta a piece of paper
un pezzo di pane a piece of bread
un piatto di a plate of
a pochi metri da a few metres from
un poco di a little; some
una porzione di a portion of
un pugno di a handful of
un quarto di a quarter of
tre quarti di three quarters of
una scatola di a tin or can of
una scodella di a bowl of
una tazza di a cup of
tutti(e) e due both of them
una zolletta di zucchero a lump of sugar

ESSENTIAL WORDS *(masculine)*

un	anello	ring
il	braccialetto	bracelet
il	deodorante	deodorant
il	gioiello	jewel
un	orologio	watch
il	pettine	comb
il	profumo	perfume
il	rasoio	razor
il	rasoio elettrico	electric shaver
lo	shampoo *(pl inv)*	shampoo
lo	spazzolino da denti	toothbrush
lo	specchio	mirror
il	trucco	make-up

USEFUL WORDS *(masculine)*

l'	acetone	nail varnish remover
un	asciugacapelli *(pl inv)*	hairdryer
il	bigodino	roller
il	ciondolo	pendant
il	dentifricio	toothpaste
il	diamante	diamond
il	dopobarba *(pl inv)*	aftershave
gli	effetti personali	personal effects
il	fard *(pl inv)*	(powder) compact
il	fazzoletto di carta	tissue
il	fondotinta *(pl inv)*	foundation
il	gemello	cufflink
il	maquillage *(pl inv)*	make-up
il	mascara *(pl inv)*	mascara
il	nécessaire da toilette *(pl inv)*	toilet bag
un	ombretto	eye shadow
un	orecchino	earring
il	pennello da barba	shaving brush
il	portachiavi *(pl inv)*	key-ring; key holder
il	rossetto	lipstick
lo	smalto per unghie	nail varnish

ESSENTIAL WORDS *(feminine)*

l'	**acqua di colonia**	eau de cologne
la	**catenina**	chain
la	**crema per il viso**	face cream
la	**spazzola**	brush

USEFUL WORDS *(feminine)*

un'	**acconciatura**	hairstyle
la	**carta igienica**	toilet paper
la	**cipria**	face powder
la	**collana**	necklace
la	**crema da barba**	shaving cream
la	**fede (nuziale)**	wedding ring
la	**manicure** *(pl inv)*	manicure
la	**perla**	pearl
la	**pettinatura**	hairstyle
la	**schiuma da barba**	shaving foam
la	**spilla**	brooch
la	**spugna**	sponge

USEFUL PHRASES

truccarsi to put on one's make-up
struccarsi to take off one's make-up
farsi un'acconciatura to do one's hair
pettinarsi to comb one's hair
spazzolarsi i capelli to brush one's hair
radersi to shave
lavarsi i denti to clean *or* brush one's teeth

ESSENTIAL WORDS (masculine)

un	albero	tree
il	fiore	flower
il	giardinaggio	gardening
il	giardiniere	gardener
il	giardino	garden
gl	ortaggi	vegetables
il	prato	lawn
il	ramo	branch
il	sole	sun
il	terreno	land; soil; ground

IMPORTANT WORDS (masculine)

il	cancello	gate
il	cespuglio	bush
il	mazzo di fiori	bunch of flowers
il	recinto	fence
il	vialetto	path; drive

USEFUL PHRASES

piantare to plant
togliere le erbacce to weed
regalare a qn un mazzo di fiori to give sb a bunch of flowers
tagliare l'erba to mow the lawn
"non calpestare" "keep off the grass"
a mio padre piace fare giardinaggio my father likes gardening

ESSENTIAL WORDS *(feminine)*

un'	**aiola**	flower bed
l'	**erba**	grass
la	**foglia**	leaf
la	**pianta**	plant
la	**pioggia** *(pl -ge)*	rain
la	**rosa**	rose
la	**terra**	soil; ground

IMPORTANT WORDS *(feminine)*

un'	**ape**	bee
la	**coltivazione**	cultivation
le	**erbacce**	weeds
l'	**ombra**	shade; shadow
la	**panchina**	bench
la	**radice**	root
la	**vespa**	wasp

USEFUL PHRASES

i fiori stanno crescendo the flowers are growing
per terra on the ground
bagnare i fiori to water the flowers
raccogliere fiori to pick flowers
andare all'ombra to go into the shade
rimanere all'ombra to remain in the shade
all'ombra di un albero in the shade of a tree

USEFUL WORDS *(masculine)*

l'	autunno	autumn
un	annaffiatoio	watering can
un	attrezzo	tool
il	bocciolo	bud
il	bucaneve *(pl inv)*	snowdrop
il	caprifoglio	honeysuckle
il	ciclamino	cyclamen
il	crisantemo	chrysanthemum
il	croco *(pl -chi)*	crocus
il	dente di leone	dandelion
il	fogliame	leaves
il	garofano	carnation
il	geranio	geranium
il	giacinto	hyacinth
il	giglio	lily
il	girasole	sunflower
l'	inverno	winter
il	lillà *(pl inv)*	lilac
il	mughetto	lily of the valley
il	narciso	daffodil
un	oleandro	oleander
un	orto	vegetable garden
il	papavero	poppy
il	raccolto	crop
il	ranuncolo	buttercup
il	rastrello	rake
il	roseto	rose bush
il	seme	seed
lo	stagno	pond
lo	stelo	stalk
il	suolo	ground; soil
il	tagliaerba *(pl inv)*	lawnmower
il	tagliasiepe *(pl inv)*	hedgecutter
il	tronco *(pl -chi)*	trunk *(of tree)*
il	tubo per annaffiare	(garden) hose
il	tulipano	tulip
il	verme	worm

USEFUL WORDS *(feminine)*

l'	azalea	azalea
l'	estate	summer
la	bacca *(pl -che)*	berry
la	begonia	begonia
la	campanula	campanula, bellflower
la	carriola	wheelbarrow
un'	edera	ivy
la	farfalla	butterfly
la	margherita	daisy
un'	orchidea	orchid
un'	ortensia	hydrangea
la	peonia	peony
la	primavera	spring
la	primula	primrose
la	rugiada	dew
la	serra	greenhouse
la	siepe	hedge
la	spina	thorn
la	stella di Natale	poinsettia
la	viola pansée	pansy
la	violetta	violet

ESSENTIAL WORDS (*masculine*)

un	**asciugamano**	towel
il	**bagnante**	swimmer
il	**battello**	passenger boat
il	**bikini** (*pl inv*)	bikini
il	**catamarano**	catamaran
il	**costume da bagno**	swimming trunks; swimsuit
il	**mare**	sea
il	**molo**	quay
il	**nuoto**	swimming
gli	**occhiali da sole**	sunglasses
il	**pescatore**	fisherman
il	**porto**	port, harbour
il	**remo**	oar

IMPORTANT WORDS (*masculine*)

il	**castello di sabbia**	sandcastle
il	**fondo**	bottom
il	**granchio**	crab
il	**lettino**	sun lounger
il	**mal di mare**	seasickness
il	**materassino gonfiabile**	airbed, lilo
l'	**orizzonte**	horizon
il	**turista**	tourist; holiday-maker
il	**windsurf** (*pl inv*)	surfboard; windsurfing

USEFUL PHRASES

in spiaggia at *or* on the beach
al mare at the seaside; at *or* on the beach
all'orizzonte on the horizon
ha il mal di mare he/she is seasick
nuotare to swim; affogare to drown
vado a fare una nuotata I'm going for a swim
tuffarsi in acqua to dive into the water
galleggiare to float

ESSENTIAL WORDS *(feminine)*

l'	abbronzatura	suntan
l'	acqua	water
la	bagnante	swimmer
la	barca *(pl -che)*	boat
la	costa	coast
un'	isola	island
la	nave	ship
la	pietra	stone
la	sabbia	sand
la	scottatura solare	sunburn
la	spiaggia *(pl -ge)*	beach

IMPORTANT WORDS *(feminine)*

la	brandina	sun lounger
la	crema solare	suncream
la	sedia a sdraio	deckchair
la	tavola da windsurf	surfboard
la	traversata	crossing
la	turista	tourist; holiday-maker

USEFUL PHRASES

in fondo al mare at the bottom of the sea
fare la traversata in barca to cross by boat
abbronzarsi to get a tan
essere nero(a) to be tanned
sa nuotare he/she can swim

USEFUL WORDS *(masculine)*

un	acquascooter *(pl inv)*	jet ski
l'	albero	mast
un	aliscafo	hydrofoil
il	bagnino	lifeguard
il	binocolo	binoculars
il	cannocchiale	telescope
il	cargo *(pl inv)*	cargo
il	ciottolo	pebble
l'	equipaggio	crew
un	estuario	estuary
il	faro	lighthouse
il	gabbiano	seagull
il	marinaio	sailor
il	motoscafo	speedboat
il	naufragio	shipwreck
un	oceano	ocean
un	ombrellone	beach umbrella
un	parasole *(pl inv)*	parasol
il	pedalò *(pl inv)*	pedalo
il	ponte	bridge
il	pontile	pier, jetty
il	promontorio	headland
il	salvagente *(pl inv)*	lifebelt
il	secchiello	bucket
il	timone	rudder
il	traghetto	ferry

USEFUL WORDS *(feminine)*

le	**alghe**	seaweed
un'	**ancora**	anchor
l'	**aria di mare**	sea air
la	**bagnina**	lifeguard
la	**baia**	bay
la	**balneazione**	bathing
la	**bandiera**	flag
la	**barca** *(pl* -che*) da diporto*	pleasure craft
la	**boa**	buoy
la	**brezza di mare**	sea breeze
la	**conchiglia**	shell
la	**corrente**	current
la	**crociera**	cruise
la	**duna di sabbia**	sand dune
la	**foce**	mouth *(of river)*
un'	**insolazione**	sunstroke
la	**marea**	tide
la	**marina**	navy; marina
la	**marinaia**	sailor
un'	**onda**	wave
la	**paletta**	spade
la	**passerella**	gangway
la	**riva**	shore
la	**roccia** *(pl* -ce*)*	rock
la	**schiuma**	foam
la	**scogliera**	cliff
la	**vela**	sail; sailing
la	**zattera**	raft

USEFUL PHRASES

mi sono preso un'insolazione **I had sunstroke**
con l'alta/la bassa marea **at low/high tide**
fare vela **to go sailing**

ESSENTIAL WORDS *(masculine)*

un	**assegno**	cheque
il	**Bancomat®** *(pl inv)*	debit card; cash machine, ATM
il	**centesimo**	cent
il	**centro commerciale**	shopping centre
il	**cliente**	customer
il	**codice a barre**	barcode
il	**commesso**	shop assistant, sales assistant
il	**denaro**	money
un	**euro** *(pl inv)*	euro
il	**fioraio**	flower shop; florist
il	**fruttivendolo**	greengrocer's
i	**grandi magazzini**	department store
un	**ipermercato**	super store
il	**libretto degli assegni**	cheque book
il	**mercato**	market
il	**negozio**	shop
il	**prezzo**	price
il	**regalo**	present, gift
il	**reparto**	department
il	**resto**	change
il	**ribasso**	reduction
i	**saldi**	sales
lo	**sconto**	discount
i	**soldi**	money
il	**supermercato**	supermarket
il	**tabaccaio**	tobacconist's; tobacconist
il	**venditore**	salesman

USEFUL PHRASES
comprare/vendere to buy/to sell
quanto costa? how much does it cost?
a quanto ammonta? how much does it come to?
l'ho pagato 20 euro I paid 20 euros for it
in macelleria/panetteria at the butcher's/bakery

ESSENTIAL WORDS (*feminine*)

un'	agenzia di viaggio	travel agent's
l'	alimentazione	food
la	banconota	banknote
la	carta di credito del negozio	store card
la	carta di credito	credit card
la	carta di debito	debit card
la	carta fedeltà	loyalty card
la	cassa	checkout; cash desk
la	cassa automatica	self-service checkout
la	cliente	customer
la	commessa	shop assistant, sales assistant
la	farmacia	chemist's
la	lista	list
la	macelleria	butcher's
la	panetteria	bakery
la	pasticceria	cake shop
la	pescheria	fishmonger's
la	posta	post office
la	profumeria	perfume shop
la	salumeria	delicatessen
la	tabaccheria	tobacconist's
la	taglia	size
la	venditrice	saleswoman

IMPORTANT WORDS (*masculine*)

un	articolo	article
il	banco (*pl* -chi)	counter
il	calzolaio	cobbler
il	commerciante	shopkeeper
il	commercio	trade
il	commercio equo e solidale	fair trade
il	direttore	manager
il	giornalaio	newsagent
il	macellaio	butcher; butcher's
il	mercatino	street market
il	mercatino delle pulci	flea market
il	negozio di generi alimentari	grocer's
il	negozio di scarpe	shoe shop
il	numero di scarpe	shoe size
il	panettiere	baker
il	parrucchiere	hairdresser; hairdresser's
il	pasticciere	confectioner
il	pescivendolo	fishmonger
il	portafoglio	wallet
il	portamonete (*pl inv*)	purse
il	reclamo	complaint
lo	scontrino	receipt

USEFUL PHRASES

sto dando un'occhiata I'm just looking
è troppo caro it's too expensive
qualcosa di più economico something cheaper
è a buon prezzo it's cheap
"pagare alla cassa" "pay at the cash desk"
vuole che le faccia un pacchetto regalo? would you like it gift-wrapped?
ci dev'essere un errore there must be some mistake

IMPORTANT WORDS *(feminine)*

la	biblioteca *(pl -che)*	library
la	borsetta	handbag
la	calcolatrice	calculator
la	commerciante	shopkeeper
la	direttrice	manager
un'	enoteca *(pl -che)*	wine shop
la	fruttivendola	fruit shop; greengrocer's
la	giornalaia	newsagent
la	libreria	bookshop
la	macellaia	butcher
la	marca *(pl -che)*	brand
la	panettiera	baker
la	parrucchiera	hairdresser
la	pasticcera	confectioner
la	pescivendola	fishmonger
la	promozione	special offer
la	pulitura (a secco)	dry-cleaner's
la	ricevuta	receipt
la	scala mobile	escalator
la	tintoria	dry-cleaner's
la	vetrina	display case; shop window

USEFUL PHRASES

qualcos'altro? anything else?

s.r.l. (= società a responsabilità limitata) limited liability company

S.p.A. (= società per azioni) joint-stock company

"in vendita qui" "on sale here"

una macchina usata a used car

in offerta on special offer

il caffè del commercio equo e solidale fair-trade coffee

USEFUL WORDS *(masculine)*

l'	**abbigliamento**	clothes
gli	**acquisti**	shopping
un	**affare**	deal
un	**agente immobiliare**	estate agent
i	**beni**	goods
il	**colore**	colour
il	**gerente**	manager
il	**gioielliere**	jeweller's
il	**libraio**	bookseller
il	**negozio di dolciumi**	sweetshop
un	**orologiaio**	watchmaker; clockmaker
un	**ottico**	optician
i	**prodotti**	produce; products
il	**prodotto**	product
lo	**sconto**	discount
il	**videonoleggio**	video shop

USEFUL PHRASES

andare a fare un giro per vetrine to go window shopping
orario di apertura opening hours
pagare in contanti to pay cash
pagare con un assegno to pay by cheque
pagare con la carta di credito to pay by credit card

USEFUL WORDS *(feminine)*

un'	agente immobiliare	estate agent
un'	agenzia di viaggio	travel agent's
un'	agenzia immobiliare	estate agent's
le	calzature	footwear
le	caramelle	sweets
la	cartoleria	stationery shop
la	cassa di risparmio	savings bank
la	coda	queue
la	commissione	errand; commission
la	droghiera	grocer
la	ferramenta	ironmonger
la	fila	queue
la	filiale	branch
la	gerente	manager
la	gioielliera	jeweller
la	lavanderia automatica	launderette
la	libraia	bookseller
le	merci	goods
un'	orologeria	watchmaker's; clockmaker's
un'	orologiaia	watchmaker; clockmaker
la	spesa	purchase; shopping
la	taglia del collo	collar size
la	vendita	sale

USEFUL PHRASES

in vetrina in the window
andare a fare acquisti to go shopping
fare la spesa to do the shopping
spendere to spend

ESSENTIAL WORDS (*masculine*)

il	basket	basketball
il	biliardo	billiards
il	calcio	football; kick
il	campionato	championship
il	campione	champion
il	campo	field; pitch; course; court
il	campo da golf	golf course
il	campo da tennis	tennis court
il	campo di calcio	football pitch
il	campo sportivo	sports field
il	ciclismo	cycling
il	cricket	cricket
il	ginnasta	gymnast
il	giocatore	player
il	gioco (*pl* -chi)	game; play
il	gol (*pl inv*)	goal
il	golf	golf
l'	hockey	hockey
il	nuoto	swimming
il	pallone	ball (*large*); football
il	risultato	result
il	rugby	rugby
gli	scacchi	chess
lo	sci (*pl inv*)	skiing; ski
lo	sci d'acqua	water skiing
lo	sport (*pl inv*)	sport
lo	stadio	stadium
il	tennis	tennis
il	windsurf (*pl inv*)	windsurfing; surfboard

USEFUL PHRASES

giocare a calcio/tennis to play football/tennis
segnare un gol/un punto to score a goal/a point
tenere il punteggio to keep the score
il campione/la campionessa del mondo the world champion
vincere/perdere una partita to win/lose a match
il mio sport preferito my favourite sport

ESSENTIAL WORDS *(feminine)*

l'	aerobica	aerobics
la	campionessa	champion
l'	equitazione	horse-riding
la	ginnasta	gymnast
la	ginnastica	gymnastics
la	giocatrice	player
la	marcia	racewalking
la	palla	ball
la	pallacanestro	basketball
la	pallavolo	volleyball
la	partita	match, game
la	pesca	fishing
la	piscina	swimming pool
la	pista	track
la	rete	net; goal
la	squadra	team
la	vela	sailing; sail

USEFUL PHRASES

pareggiare to equalize; to draw

correre to run; saltare to jump; lanciare to throw

battere qn to beat sb

allenarsi to train

il Liverpool conduce per 2 a 1 Liverpool is leading by 2 goals to 1

un partita a tennis a game of tennis

è socio di un club he belongs to a club

andare a pesca to go fishing

andare in piscina to go to the swimming pool

sai (or sa) nuotare? can you swim?

fare sport to do sport

andare in bicicletta to go cycling

fare vela to go sailing

fare jogging/alpinismo to go jogging/climbing

pattini da ghiaccio/a rotelle (ice) skate/roller skates

pattini in linea Rollerblades®

tiro con l'arco/al bersaglio archery/target practice

IMPORTANT WORDS (*masculine*)

un	arbitro	referee; umpire (*tennis*)
un	incontro	match
il	punteggio	score
il	torneo	tournament

USEFUL WORDS (*masculine*)

un	allenatore	trainer; coach
l'	alpinismo	mountaineering
un	avversario	opponent
il	canottaggio	rowing
il	cronometro	stopwatch
il	giavellotto	javelin
i	Giochi Olimpici	Olympic Games
l'	intervallo	half-time
l'	ippodromo	race course
il	jogging	jogging
il	parapendio	paragliding
il	pattinaggio su ghiaccio	(ice) skating
il	pattino	skate
il	perdente	loser
il	portiere	goalkeeper
il	principiante	beginner
il	pugilato	boxing
il	punto	point
il	remo	oar
il	salto in alto	high jump
il	salto in lungo	long jump
lo	spettatore	spectator
lo	squash	squash
i	tempi supplementari	extra time
il	tiro	shooting
i	tuffi	diving
il	vincitore	winner
il	volano	shuttlecock; badminton

IMPORTANT WORDS *(feminine)*

l'	atletica	athletics
le	bocce	pétanque
la	boxe	boxing
la	Coppa del Mondo	World Cup
la	corsa	race
le	corse dei cavalli	horse-racing
la	difesa	defence
l'	ippica	horse-racing
le	Olimpiadi	Olympic Games
la	pallina	ball *(small)*
la	pista da sci	ski slope
la	slitta	sledge

USEFUL WORDS *(feminine)*

un'	allenatrice	trainer, coach
un'	avversaria	opponent
la	canna da pesca	fishing rod
un'	eliminatoria	heat
la	finale	final
la	lotta libera	wrestling
la	maglietta	jersey, shirt
la	perdente	loser
la	pesca	fishing
la	pista da pattinaggio	skating rink
la	pista da pattinaggio su ghiaccio	ice rink
la	principiante	beginner
la	racchetta da ping pong	ping pong bat
la	racchetta da sci	ski pole
la	racchetta da tennis	tennis racket
le	scarpe da ginnastica	sports shoes; trainers
le	scarpe da tennis	tennis shoes
la	scherma	fencing
la	spettatrice	spectator
la	stazione sciistica	ski resort
la	tappa	stage
la	tribuna	stand
la	vincitrice	winner

ESSENTIAL WORDS (*masculine*)

un	**attore**	actor
un	**auditorium** (*pl inv*)	auditorium
il	**biglietto**	ticket
il	**botteghino**	box office
il	**cinema** (*pl inv*)	cinema
il	**circo** (*pl -chi*)	circus
il	**clown** (*pl inv*)	clown
il	**comico**	comedian
il	**costume**	costume
il	**film** (*pl inv*)	film
il	**pagliaccio**	clown
il	**posto (a sedere)**	seat
il	**programma**	programme
il	**pubblico**	audience; public
il	**sipario**	curtain
lo	**spettacolo**	show; performance; showing
il	**teatro**	theatre
il	**western** (*pl inv*)	western

IMPORTANT WORDS (*masculine*)

il	**balletto**	ballet
il	**cartellone**	poster; playbill
un	**intervallo**	interval
il	**primo attore**	leading man

USEFUL PHRASES

andare a teatro/al cinema to go to the theatre/to the cinema
prenotare un posto to book a seat
una poltrona in platea a seat in the stalls
il mio attore preferito/la mia attrice preferita my favourite actor/actress
durante l'intervallo during the interval
entrare in scena to come on stage
interpretare la parte di to play the part of

ESSENTIAL WORDS *(feminine)*

l'	atmosfera	atmosphere
un'	attrice	actress
la	colonna sonora	soundtrack
la	commedia	play; comedy
la	galleria	the circle
la	musica *(pl -che)*	music
l'	opera	opera
un'	orchestra	orchestra
la	pagliaccia *(pl -ce)*	clown
la	pellicola	film
la	platea	stalls
la	poltrona	seat
la	prima galleria	dress circle
la	proiezione	screening *(of film)*
la	sala	screen *(of cinema)*
la	star *(m+f pl inv)*	film star
la	tragedia	tragedy
un'	uscita	exit

USEFUL PHRASES

recitare to play
ballare to dance
cantare to sing
girare un film to shoot a film
"versione originale" "original version"
"con sottotitoli" "subtitled"
"tutto esaurito" "sold out"
applaudire to clap
bis! encore!
bravo! bravo!
un film di fantascienza/d'amore a science fiction film/a romance
un film d'avventura/dell'orrore an adventure/horror film

IMPORTANT WORDS *(masculine continued)*

il	**protagonista**	protagonist; star
il	**sottotitolo**	subtitle
il	**titolo**	title
il	**trucco** *(pl -chi)*	make-up; trick

USEFUL WORDS *(masculine)*

gli	**applausi**	applause
il	**cast** *(pl inv)*	cast
il	**commediografo**	playwright
il	**copione**	script
il	**critico**	critic
il	**direttore artistico**	artistic director
il	**direttore di scena**	stage manager
il	**drammaturgo** *(pl -ghi)*	playwright
il	**guardaroba** *(pl inv)*	cloakroom
il	**loggione**	the "gods"
il	**musical** *(pl inv)*	musical
il	**palco** *(pl -chi)*	box
il	**palco(scenico)**	stage
il	**personaggio**	character
il	**produttore**	producer
il	**regista**	director *(cinema)*; producer *(TV)*
il	**ridotto**	foyer
il	**riflettore**	spotlight
il	**ruolo**	part
il	**serial** *(pl inv)*	serial
lo	**scenario**	scenery; set
lo	**sceneggiatore**	scriptwriter
lo	**schermo**	screen
lo	**spettatore**	member of the audience
il	**suggeritore**	prompter

IMPORTANT WORDS *(feminine)*

la	locandina	poster
un'	imbeccata	cue; prompt
la	maschera	usher; usherette
la	prenotazione	booking
la	prima attrice	leading lady
la	protagonista	protagonist; star

USEFUL WORDS *(feminine)*

la	biglietteria	ticket office
la	buca *(pl -che)* dell'orchestra	orchestra pit
la	commediografa	playwright
la	critica *(pl -che)*	review; critics
la	direttrice di scena	stage manager
la	drammaturga *(pl -ghe)*	playwright
la	farsa	farce
le	luci della ribalta	footlights
la	messa in scena	production
la	parte	part
la	piccionaia	the "gods"
la	prima	first night, premiere
la	produttrice	producer
la	produzione	production
le	prove	(dress) rehearsal
le	quinte	wings
la	rappresentazione	performance
la	recitazione	acting
la	regista	director *(cinema)*; producer *(TV)*
la	scena	scene
la	sceneggiatrice	scriptwriter
la	sceneggiatura	script
la	scenografia	set design
la	serie *(pl inv)*	series
la	soap *(pl inv)*	soap (opera)
la	spettatrice	member of the audience
la	suggeritrice	prompter
la	trama	plot
la	videoclip *(pl inv)*	music video

ESSENTIAL WORDS (*masculine*)

un	**anno**	year
il	**fine settimana** (*pl inv*)	weekend
il	**giorno**	day
un	**istante**	moment; instant
il	**mattino**	morning
il	**mese**	month
il	**minuto**	minute
il	**momento**	moment
un	**orologio**	watch; clock
il	**pomeriggio**	afternoon; evening
il	**quarto d'ora**	quarter of an hour
il	**secolo**	century
il	**secondo**	second
il	**tempo**	time

USEFUL PHRASES

a mezzogiorno at midday

a mezzanotte at midnight

oggi today

domani tomorrow

dopodomani the day after tomorrow

ieri yesterday

ieri sera last night, yesterday evening

l'altroieri the day before yesterday

due giorni fa 2 days ago

tra due giorni in 2 days

una settimana a week

quindici giorni a fortnight

ogni giorno every day

che giorno è oggi? what day is it?; what's the date?

al momento at the moment

le tre meno un quarto a quarter to 3

le tre e un quarto a quarter past 3

oggigiorno nowadays

il ventunesimo secolo in the 21st century

ESSENTIAL WORDS (feminine)

la	**giornata**	day
la	**mattina**	morning
la	**mezzora**	half an hour
la	**notte**	night
un'	**ora**	hour
la	**sera**	night; evening
la	**serata**	evening
la	**settimana**	week
la	**sveglia**	alarm clock

USEFUL PHRASES

l'anno scorso/prossimo last/next year
la prossima settimana next week
entro mezzora in half an hour
una volta once
due/tre volte two/three times
diverse volte several times
tre volte all'anno three times a year
nove volte su dieci nine times out of ten
c'era una volta once upon a time there was
dieci alla volta ten at a time
che ora è? what time is it?
sai (or sa) che ora è? have you got the time?
sono le sei/le sei meno dieci/le sei e mezza it is 6 o'clock/10 to 6/half past 6
sono le due in punto it is 2 o'clock exactly
poco fa a while ago
tra un po' in a while
presto early
tardi late
stanotte last night (past); tonight (to come)

IMPORTANT WORDS *(masculine)*

il **futuro**	future; future tense
il **giorno dopo**	next day
il **passato**	past; past tense
il **presente**	present *(time)*; present tense
il **ritardo**	delay

USEFUL WORDS *(masculine)*

un **anno bisestile**	leap year
il **calendario**	calendar
il **cronometro**	stopwatch
il **decennio**	decade
il **Medio Evo**	Middle Ages
un **orologio a pendolo**	grandfather clock
un **orologio da polso**	wristwatch
il **quadrante**	face *(of clock)*
il **sorgere del sole**	sunrise
il **tramonto**	sunset

USEFUL PHRASES

due giorni dopo two days later
il giorno prima the day before
ogni secondo giorno every other day
in futuro in the future
un giorno di ferie a day off
un giorno festivo a public holiday
un giorno lavorativo a weekday
in un giorno di pioggia on a rainy day
all'alba at dawn
la mattina/sera seguente the following morning/evening
adesso now

USEFUL WORDS *(feminine)*

l'	**alba**	dawn
un'	**epoca** *(pl -che)*	time; era
le	**lancette**	hands *(of clock)*
la	**vigilia**	eve

USEFUL PHRASES

sei *(or* è*)* in ritardo **you are late**
sei *(or* è*)* in anticipo **you are early**
quest'orologio va avanti/indietro **this watch is fast/slow**
arrivare puntuale **to arrive on time**
quanto tempo? **how long?**
nel terzo millennio **the third millennium**
dormire fino a tardi **to have a lie-in**
da un momento all'altro **any minute now**
tra una settimana **in a week's time**
lunedì otto **a week on Monday**
la notte prima **the night before**
a quel tempo **at that time**

ESSENTIAL WORDS (*masculine*)

il **bricolage**	DIY
il **fai da te**	DIY
un **attrezzo**	tool

USEFUL WORDS (*masculine*)

un **ago** (*pl* -ghi)	needle
il **badile**	spade
il **cacciavite** (*pl inv*)	screwdriver
il **chiodo**	nail
un **elastico**	rubber band
il **filo spinato**	(barbed) wire
il **forcone**	(garden) fork
il **lucchetto**	padlock
il **martello**	hammer
il **martello pneumatico**	pneumatic drill
il **metro a nastro**	tape measure
il **nastro adesivo**	sticky tape
il **pennello**	paintbrush
il **piccone**	pickaxe
lo **scalpello**	chisel
lo **scotch** (*pl inv*)	Sellotape®
il **secchio**	bucket
il **trapano**	drill
il **tuttofare** (*pl inv*)	handyman

USEFUL PHRASES

fare qualche lavoretto to do odd jobs
battere un chiodo con il martello to hammer in a nail
"pittura fresca" "wet paint"
pitturare to paint
mettere la carta da parati to wallpaper

ESSENTIAL WORDS *(feminine)*

la	chiave	key
la	chiave inglese	spanner
la	corda	rope
la	macchina	machine
un'	officina	workshop

USEFUL WORDS *(feminine)*

la	batteria	battery
la	carta vetrata	sandpaper
la	cassetta degli attrezzi	toolbox
la	colla	glue
le	forbici	scissors
un'	impalcatura	scaffolding
la	lima	file
la	molla	spring
la	pala	shovel
la	pila	battery *(in radio etc)*; torch
le	pinze	pliers
la	puntina da disegno	drawing pin
la	scala (a libretto)	(step)ladder
la	sega *(pl -ghe)*	saw
la	serratura	lock
la	tavola (di legno)	plank
la	tuttofare *(pl inv)*	handywoman
la	vernice *(pl inv)*	varnish
la	vite	screw

USEFUL PHRASES

"lavori in corso: vietato l'accesso" "construction site: keep out"
pratico(a) handy
tagliare to cut
riparare to mend
avvitare to screw (in)
svitare to unscrew

ESSENTIAL WORDS *(masculine)*

un **abitante**	inhabitant
un **albergo** *(pl -ghi)*	hotel
un **angolo**	corner
un **autobus** *(pl inv)*	bus
il **caffè** *(pl inv)*	café; coffee
il **centro (della città)**	town centre
il **cinema** *(pl inv)*	cinema
il **commissariato di polizia**	police station
il **comune**	town hall
il **condominio**	block of flats
i **dintorni**	surroundings
il **distributore di benzina**	petrol station
il **duomo**	cathedral
un **edificio**	building
il **giro**	tour
l' **inquinamento (dell'aria)**	(air) pollution
il **mercato**	market
il **municipio**	town hall
il **museo**	museum; art gallery
il **negozio**	shop
il **parcheggio**	car park; parking space
il **parco** *(pl -chi)*	park
il **pedone**	pedestrian
il **poliziotto**	policeman
il **ponte**	bridge
il **posteggio dei taxi**	taxi rank
il **quartiere**	district
il **quartiere degradato**	slum area
il **ristorante**	restaurant
il **sobborgo** *(pl -ghi)*	suburb
il **taxi** *(pl inv)*	taxi
il **teatro**	theatre
il **turista**	tourist
un **ufficio**	office
un **ufficio postale**	post office

ESSENTIAL WORDS *(feminine)*

un'	abitante	inhabitant
un'	automobile	car
la	banca *(pl -che)*	bank
la	casa popolare	council house
la	cattedrale	cathedral
la	città *(pl inv)*	town, city
la	corriera	bus; coach
la	fabbrica *(pl -che)*	factory
la	fermata dell'autobus	bus stop
la	lavanderia automatica	launderette
la	macchina	car
la	metropolitana	underground, subway
la	panchina	bench
la	piazza	square
la	piscina	swimming pool
la	polizia	police
la	poliziotta	policewoman
la	posta	post office
la	stazione (ferroviaria)	(train) station
la	stazione delle corriere	bus station
la	strada	road
la	torre	tower
la	turista	tourist
la	via	street
la	vista	view

USEFUL PHRASES

vado in città I'm going into town
in centro in the town centre
nella piazza in the square
una strada a senso unico a one-way street
"vietato l'accesso" "no entry"
attraversare la strada to cross the road

IMPORTANT WORDS *(masculine)*

un	abbonamento	season ticket
un	agente di polizia	police officer
il	cartello	notice; sign
il	castello	castle
il	centro storico	old town
il	distributore di biglietti	ticket machine
il	giardino pubblico	park
il	giornalaio	news stand
un	incrocio	crossroads
un	ingorgo *(pl -ghi)*	traffic jam
un	internet caffè *(pl inv)*	internet café
il	marciapiedi *(pl inv)*	pavement
il	monumento	monument
il	parchimetro	parking meter
il	parco *(pl -chi)*	park
il	passante	passer-by
il	posto	place
il	semaforo	traffic lights
il	sindaco	mayor
il	supermercato	supermarket
il	traffico	traffic
lo	zoo *(pl inv)*	zoo

USEFUL PHRASES

all'angolo della strada **at the corner of the street**
vivere in periferia **to live in the outskirts**
camminare **to walk**
prendere l'autobus/la metropolitana **to take the bus/the underground**
comprare un biglietto multicorse **to buy a multiple-journey ticket**
timbrare il biglietto **to punch the ticket**

IMPORTANT WORDS *(feminine)*

un'	agente di polizia	police officer
la	biblioteca *(pl -che)*	library
la	chiesa	church
la	circolazione	traffic
la	città vecchia	old town
la	deviazione	diversion
un'	edicola	newspaper kiosk
la	moschea	mosque
la	passante	passer-by
la	pinacoteca	art gallery
la	sinagoga *(pl -ghe)*	synagogue
la	stazione di servizio	petrol station
la	via principale	main street
la	zona	zone; area
la	zona a traffico limitato	restricted traffic zone
la	zona industriale	industrial estate
la	zona pedonale	pedestrian precinct

USEFUL PHRASES

industriale industrial
storico(a) historic
bello(a) pretty
brutto(a) ugly
pulito(a) clean
sporco(a) dirty

USEFUL WORDS *(masculine)*

un	attraversamento pedonale	pedestrian crossing
il	bar *(pl inv)*	café-bar
il	bastione	rampart
il	caffè *(pl inv)*	coffee shop, café
il	carcere	prison
il	cartello stradale	road sign
il	cimitero	cemetery
il	ciottolo	cobblestone
il	cittadino	citizen
il	consiglio comunale	town council
il	dépliant *(pl inv)*	leaflet
il	distretto	district
il	furgone dei traslochi	delivery van
il	grattacielo	skyscraper
il	lampione	street lamp
i	luoghi d'interesse	sights, places of interest
il	manifestino	leaflet
il	passeggino	pushchair
il	quartiere residenziale	residential area
il	sondaggio d'opinione	opinion poll
il	vicolo cieco *(pl -i -chi)*	cul-de-sac, dead end
il	volantino	flyer, leaflet

USEFUL WORDS *(feminine)*

la	carrozzina	pram
la	caserma dei pompieri	fire station
la	cittadina	citizen
la	coda	queue
la	curva	bend
la	fermata dell'autobus	bus stop
la	fognatura	sewer
la	folla	crowd
la	freccia *(pl* -ce)	arrow
la	galleria d'arte	art gallery
un'	isola pedonale	traffic island
la	periferia	outskirts
la	pista ciclabile	cycle path; cycle lane
la	popolazione	population
la	prigione	prison
la	processione	procession
la	sfilata	parade
la	statua	statue
la	strada senza uscita	cul-de-sac, dead end
le	strisce pedonali	zebra crossing
la	superficie stradale	road surface

ESSENTIAL WORDS *(masculine)*

un	armadietto per i bagagli	left-luggage locker
l'	arrivo	arrival
il	bagaglio	luggage
il	bar della stazione	station buffet
il	biglietto	ticket
il	biglietto di andata e ritorno	return ticket
il	biglietto di sola andata	single ticket
il	binario	platform; track
il	buffet della stazione *(pl inv)*	station buffet
il	deposito bagagli	left-luggage office
il	doganiere	customs officer
il	facchino	porter
il	freno	brake
un	intercity *(pl inv)*	intercity train
il	numero	number
un	orario	timetable
il	parcheggio dei taxi	taxi rank
il	passaporto	passport
il	ponte	bridge
il	portafoglio	wallet
il	posto (a sedere)	seat
il	ritardo	delay
lo	scompartimento	compartment
lo	scontrino	ticket; receipt
il	supplemento	extra charge *(to be paid on intercity)*
il	taxi *(pl inv)*	taxi
il	treno	train
il	treno ad alta velocità	high-speed train
il	treno regionale	local stopping train
un	ufficio oggetti smarriti	lost property office
il	vagone	carriage
il	viaggiatore	traveller
il	viaggio	journey

ESSENTIAL WORDS *(feminine)*

la	bici *(pl inv)*	bike
la	bicicletta	bicycle
la	biglietteria	ticket office
la	borsa	bag
la	borsetta	handbag
la	cartina stradale	map
la	classe	class
la	coincidenza	connection
la	direzione	direction
la	dogana	customs
la	doganiera	customs officer
la	fermata della metropolitana	underground station
le	informazioni	information
la	linea	line
la	metropolitana	underground, subway
la	partenza	departure
la	prenotazione	reservation
la	riduzione	reduction
la	sala d'aspetto	waiting room
la	stazione	station
la	tariffa	fare
la	valigia *(pl -gie or -ge)*	suitcase
la	viaggiatrice	traveller

USEFUL PHRASES

prenotare un posto to book a seat

pagare un supplemento to pay an extra charge, to pay a surcharge

fare/disfare i bagagli to pack/unpack

IMPORTANT WORDS *(masculine)*

un	**allarme**	alarm
il	**cancello**	barrier
il	**carnet di biglietti** *(pl inv)*	book of tickets
il	**confine**	border
il	**controllore**	ticket collector
il	**guidatore**	driver
il	**vagone letto** *(pl -i ~)*	sleeping car
il	**vagone ristorante** *(pl -i ~)*	dining car

USEFUL WORDS *(masculine)*

un	**abbonamento**	season ticket
il	**bagagliaio**	trunk
il	**capostazione** *(pl capistazione)*	stationmaster
il	**deragliamento**	derailment
il	**fischietto**	whistle
il	**macchinista**	engine-driver
il	**passaggio a livello**	level crossing
il	**tabellone**	noticeboard
il	**treno merci** *(pl -i ~)*	goods train
il	**vagone**	carriage
il	**viaggio**	journey; trip

USEFUL PHRASES

prendere il treno to take the train
perdere il treno to miss the train
convalidare il biglietto to date stamp a ticket
salire in treno to get on the train
scendere dal treno to get off the train
è libero questo posto? is this seat free?
il treno è in ritardo the train is late
"è vietato sporgersi dal finestrino" "do not lean out of the window"

IMPORTANT WORDS *(feminine)*

la	carrozza	carriage
la	cuccetta	couchette
la	destinazione	destination
la	durata	length (of time)
la	ferrovia	railway
la	frontiera	border
la	mancia *(pl -ce)*	tip
la	scala mobile	escalator
la	tariffa	fare
	Trenitalia	Italian Railway

USEFUL WORDS *(feminine)*

la	capostazione *(pl inv)*	stationmaster
un'	etichetta	label
la	locomotiva	locomotive
la	macchinista	engine-driver
le	rotaie	rails

USEFUL PHRASES

vengo con te alla stazione I'll go to the station with you
ti accompagno alla stazione I'll take you to the station
vengo a prenderti alla stazione I'll come and pick you up at the station
il treno delle dieci diretto a/proveniente da Roma the 10 o'clock train to/
  from Rome

ESSENTIAL WORDS *(masculine)*

un	albero	tree
il	bosco *(pl -chi)*	wood
il	ramo	branch

USEFUL WORDS *(masculine)*

un	abete	fir tree
un	acero	maple
un	agrifoglio	holly
un	albero da frutta	fruit tree
un	albicocco *(pl -chi)*	apricot tree
un	arancio	orange tree; orange
un	arbusto	shrub
il	fico *(pl -chi)*	fig tree; fig
il	leccio	ilex, holm oak
il	banano	banana tree
il	biancospino	hawthorn
il	bocciolo	bud
il	bosso	box tree
il	castagno	chestnut tree
il	cespuglio	bush
il	ciliegio	cherry tree
il	faggio	beech
il	fogliame	foliage
il	frassino	ash
il	limone	lemon tree; lemon
il	melo	apple tree
il	noce	walnut tree
un	olmo	elm
un	orto	orchard
il	pero	pear tree
il	pesco *(pl -chi)*	peach tree
il	pino	pine
il	pioppo	poplar
il	platano	plane tree
il	rovere	oak
il	salice piangente	weeping willow
il	tiglio	lime tree
il	tronco *(pl -chi)*	trunk

ESSENTIAL WORDS *(feminine)*

la	**foglia**	leaf
la	**foresta**	forest
la	**foresta pluviale**	rain forest
la	**palma**	palm tree

USEFUL WORDS *(feminine)*

la	**bacca** *(pl -che)*	berry
la	**betulla**	birch
la	**corteccia** *(pl -ce)*	bark
la	**foresta**	forest
la	**gemma**	bud
la	**radice**	root
la	**vigna**	vineyard

ESSENTIAL WORDS *(masculine)*

l'	aglio	garlic
il	cavolfiore	cauliflower
i	fagiolini	French beans
i	funghi	mushrooms
gli	ortaggi	vegetables
il	peperone	pepper
i	piselli	peas
il	pomodoro	tomato

USEFUL WORDS *(masculine)*

un	asparago	asparagus
il	basilico	basil
i	broccoli	broccoli
il	carciofo	artichoke
i	cavoletti di Bruxelles	Brussels sprouts
il	cavolo	cabbage
i	ceci	chickpeas
il	cetriolo	cucumber
il	cipollotto	spring onion
i	fagioli	beans
i	fagioli bianchi	haricot beans
i	(fagioli) borlotti	kidney beans
i	legumi	pulses
il	mais	sweetcorn
il	porro	leek
il	prezzemolo	parsley
il	ravanello	radish
il	sedano	celery
gli	spinaci	spinach

USEFUL PHRASES

coltivare ortaggi to grow vegetables
una pannocchia bollita corn on the cob

ESSENTIAL WORDS *(feminine)*

la	**carota**	carrot
la	**cipolla**	onion
l'	**insalata**	salad
la	**patata**	potato
le	**verdure**	vegetables

USESFUL WORDS *(feminine)*

la	**barbabietola**	beetroot
la	**cicoria**	chicory
l'	**indivia**	endive
la	**lattuga**	lettuce
le	**lenticchie**	lentils
la	**melanzana**	aubergine
la	**rapa**	turnip
la	**scarola**	curly endive
la	**zucca** *(pl* **-che***)*	pumpkin
la	**zucchina**	courgette

USEFUL PHRASES

carote grattugiate grated carrot
biologico(a) organic
vegetariano(a) vegetarian

ESSENTIAL WORDS *(masculine)*

un	**aereo**	plane
un	**aeroplano**	aeroplane
un	**autobus** *(pl inv)*	bus
il	**camion** *(pl inv)*	lorry
il	**camper** *(pl inv)*	camper van
il	**casco** *(pl -chi)*	helmet
il	**ciclomotore**	moped
un	**elicottero**	helicopter
il	**ferry** *(pl inv)*	ferry
il	**furgone**	van
il	**mezzo di trasporto**	means of transport
il	**motorino**	moped
il	**prezzo del biglietto**	fare
lo	**scooter** *(pl inv)*	scooter
il	**taxi** *(pl inv)*	taxi
il	**tir** *(pl inv)*	heavy goods vehicle
il	**traghetto**	ferry
i	**trasporti pubblici**	public transport
il	**treno**	train
il	**veicolo**	vehicle
il	**veliero**	sailing ship

IMPORTANT WORDS *(masculine)*

il	**camion** *(pl inv)* **dei pompieri**	fire engine
il	**carro attrezzi**	breakdown van

USEFUL PHRASES

viaggiare to travel
ha preso un aereo per Palermo he/she flew to Palermo
prendere l'autobus/la metropolitana/il treno to take the bus/the subway/
   the train
andare in bicicletta to go cycling
ci si può andare in macchina you can go there by car

ESSENTIAL WORDS *(feminine)*

un'	**auto** *(pl inv)*	car
un'	**automobile**	car
la	**barca** *(pl -che)*	boat
la	**barca** *(pl -che)* **a remi**	rowing boat
la	**barca** *(pl -che)* **a vela**	sailing boat
la	**bici** *(pl inv)*	bike
la	**bicicletta**	bicycle
la	**corriera**	coach
la	**distanza**	distance
la	**funicolare**	funicular railway
la	**macchina**	car
la	**metropolitana**	underground, subway
la	**moto** *(pl inv)*	motorbike
la	**motocicletta**	motorcycle, motorbike
la	**parte anteriore**	front
la	**parte posteriore**	back
la	**roulotte** *(pl inv)*	caravan
la	**vespa®**	vespa®

IMPORTANT WORDS *(feminine)*

un'	**ambulanza**	ambulance
un'	**autopompa**	fire engine

USEFUL PHRASES

riparare la macchina a qn to repair sb's car
una macchina a noleggio a hire car
una macchina sportiva a sports car
una macchina da corsa a racing car
la macchina della ditta the company car
"auto usate" "used cars"
partire to start, to move off
to sit in the front/back sedersi davanti/dietro

USEFUL WORDS *(masculine)*

un	**aliante**	glider
un	**aliscafo**	hydrofoil
un	**autoarticolato**	articulated lorry
un	**autocarro**	lorry
il	**bulldozer** *(pl inv)*	bulldozer
il	**camion cisterna** *(pl inv)*	tanker lorry
il	**carro**	cart
il	**carro armato**	tank
il	**disco volante** *(pl -chi -i)*	flying saucer
il	**fuoristrada** *(pl inv)*	jeep, off-road vehicle
il	**furgone dei traslochi**	delivery van
il	**gommone**	rubber dinghy
un	**hovercraft** *(pl inv)*	hovercraft
un	**idrovolante**	seaplane
il	**motore**	engine
il	**motoscafo**	speedboat
il	**passeggino**	pushchair
il	**razzo**	rocket
il	**rimorchiatore**	tug
il	**rimorchio**	trailer
il	**sottomarino**	submarine
il	**suv** *(pl inv)*	suv
il	**tram** *(pl inv)*	tram
il	**trattore**	tractor
un	**ufo** *(pl inv)*	UFO *(unidentified flying object)*
lo	**yacht** *(pl inv)*	yacht

USEFUL WORDS *(feminine)*

un'	astronave	spaceship
una	barca *(pl -che)* da diporto	pleasure boat
la	canoa	canoe
la	carrozzina	pram
la	chiatta	barge
la	funivia	cable car
un'	imbarcazione	boat
la	jeep *(pl inv)*	jeep
la	lancia *(pl -ce)*	launch
la	lancia *(pl -ce)* di salvataggio	lifeboat
la	locomotiva	locomotive
la	macchina familiare	estate car
la	monovolume *(pl inv)*	people carrier
la	nave	ship
la	nave cisterna *(pl -i ~)*	tanker (ship); water supply ship
la	navetta	shuttle bus
la	petroliera	oil tanker *(ship)*
la	portaerei *(pl inv)*	aircraft carrier
la	seggiovia	chairlift
la	station wagon *(pl inv)*	estate car

ESSENTIAL WORDS *(masculine)*

l'	autunno	autumn
il	bollettino meteo	weather report
il	calore	heat
il	cielo	sky
il	clima	climate
l'	est	east
il	freddo	cold
il	grado	degree
il	ghiaccio	ice
l'	inverno	winter
il	meteo *(pl inv)*	weather report
il	nord	north
l'	ovest	west
un	ombrello	umbrella
il	sole	sun; sunshine
il	sud	south
il	tempo	weather
il	vento	wind

USEFUL PHRASES

che tempo fa? **what's the weather like?**
fa caldo/freddo **it's hot/cold**
è una bella giornata **it's a lovely day**
è una brutta giornata **it's a horrible day**
all'aria aperta **in the open air**
c'è nebbia **it's foggy**
30° all'ombra **30° in the shade**
ascoltare le previsioni del tempo **to listen to the weather forecast**
piovere **to rain**
nevicare **to snow**
c'è il sole **it's sunny**
c'è vento **it's windy**
piove **it's raining**
nevica **it's snowing**

ESSENTIAL WORDS *(feminine)*

l'	aria	air
l'	estate	summer
la	nebbia	fog
la	neve	snow
la	nuvola	cloud
la	pioggia *(pl -ge)*	rain
le	previsioni del tempo	(weather) forecast
la	primavera	spring
la	regione	region, area
la	stagione	season
la	temperatura	temperature

USEFUL PHRASES

brilla il sole **the sun is shining**
soffia il vento **the wind is blowing**
si gela **it's freezing**
gelare **to freeze**
c'è stata una gelata **there's been a frost**
sciogliersi **to melt**
una giornata di sole **a sunny day**
una giornata di pioggia **a rainy day**
tempestoso(a) **stormy**
fresco(a) **cool**
variabile **changeable**
umido(a) **humid**
è coperto **the sky is overcast**

IMPORTANT WORDS (*masculine*)

il	buio	darkness
il	fumo	smoke
il	rovescio	shower

USEFUL WORDS (*masculine*)

un	acquazzone	downpour
un	arcobaleno	rainbow
il	barometro	barometer
il	cambiamento	change
il	chiaro di luna	moonlight
il	crepuscolo	nightfall, dusk
il	cumulo di neve	snowdrift
il	disgelo	thaw
il	fiocco (*pl* -chi) di neve	snowflake
il	fulmine	flash of lightning
il	ghiacciolo	icicle
il	miglioramento	improvement
il	parafulmine (*pl inv*)	lightning conductor
il	raggio di sole	ray of sunshine
lo	spazzaneve (*pl inv*)	snowplough
il	temporale	thunderstorm
il	tramonto	sunset
il	tuono	thunder
un	uragano	hurricane

IMPORTANT WORDS *(feminine)*

la **burrasca** *(pl -che)*	storm
la **polvere**	dust
le **precipitazioni**	rainfall
la **schiarita**	sunny spell
la **tempesta**	storm
la **tormenta**	storm
la **tromba d'aria**	whirlwind
la **visibilità**	visibility

USEFUL WORDS *(feminine)*

l' **alba**	dawn, daybreak
un' **alluvione**	flood
l' **atmosfera**	atmosphere
la **brezza**	breeze
la **brina**	frost *(on the ground)*
la **corrente (d'aria)**	draught
la **foschia**	mist
la **gelata**	frost
la **goccia di pioggia**	raindrop
la **grandine**	hail
un' **inondazione**	flood
la **nevicata**	snowfall
un' **ondata di caldo**	heatwave
l' **oscurità**	darkness
la **pozzanghera**	puddle
la **raffica di vento**	gust of wind
la **rugiada**	dew
la **siccità**	drought

ESSENTIAL WORDS (*masculine*)

il	bagno	bathroom
il	bidone delle immondizie	dustbin
il	dormitorio	dormitory
i	gabinetti	lavatories
il	lenzuolo (*pl f* lenzuola)	sheet
i	letti a castello	bunk bed
il	letto	bed
il	listino dei prezzi	price list
un	ospite	visitor
un	ostello della gioventù	youth hostel
il	pasto	meal
il	rifugio	mountain hostel
i	servizi	toilets
il	silenzio	silence
il	soggiorno	stay; living room
un	ufficio	office

IMPORTANT WORDS (*masculine*)

il	lavandino	washbasin
il	regolamento	rules
il	sacco (*pl* -chi) a pelo	sleeping bag
lo	zaino	rucksack

ESSENTIAL WORDS *(feminine)*

la	cartina	map
la	colazione	breakfast
la	cucina	kitchen; cooking
la	doccia *(pl -ce)*	shower
le	lenzuola	sheets
la	notte	night
un'	ospite	visitor
la	sala giochi	games room
la	stanza da pranzo	dining room
la	tariffa	rate
le	toilette	toilets
le	vacanze	holidays

IMPORTANT WORDS *(feminine)*

la	biancheria del letto	bed linen
la	camminata	walk
un'	escursione	hike; trip
la	guida	guidebook; guide
la	tessera (associativa)	membership card

USEFUL PHRASES

passare una notte in un ostello to spend a night at the youth hostel
vorrei comprare un sacco a pelo I would like to buy a sleeping bag
non c'è più posto there's no more room

The vocabulary items on pages 204 to 242 have been grouped under parts of speech rather than topics because they can apply in a wide range of circumstances. Use them just as freely as the vocabulary already given.

ARTICLES AND PRONOUNS

> **What is an article?**
> An **article** is one of the words *the*, *a* and *an* which is given in front of a noun.

> **What is a pronoun?**
> A **pronoun** is a word you use instead of a noun, when you do not need or want to name someone or something directly, for example, *it*, *you*, *none*.

alcuni/alcune some
altrettanto the same
altro/altra: un altro/un'altra
  another one
  altri/altre others
  gli altri/le altre other people
ambedue both
che what; which; that
chi who; whoever
chiunque whoever; anyone
ci us; to us; ourselves; each other
ciascuno/ciascuna each
ciò this
cui to whom; of whom; whose
egli he
entrambi both
essi/esse they
esso/a it
gli the; him; to him; it; to it
i the
il the
io I
la the; her; it; you
le the; her; to her; to you; them

lei she; her; you
li them
lo the; him; it
loro they; them; theirs
lui he; him
me me; to me
mi me; to me; myself
mio/mia/miei/mie: il mio/la mia/
  i miei/le mie mine
ne of it; of them; about it; about
  them
nessuno/nessuna nobody; no-one;
  none; anyone
niente nothing
noi we; us
nostro/nostra/nostri/nostre:
  il nostro/la nostra/i nostri/le
  nostre ours
nulla nothing; anything
ognuno each; everbody
parecchio/parecchia quite a lot
qualcosa something; anything
qualcuno somebody; someone;
  anybody; anyone

qual(e) which; what
quanti/quante how many
quanto/quanta how much
quelli/quelle/quegli those ones
quello/quella that one
questi/queste these ones
questo/questa this one
sé himself; herself; itself;
   themselves; oneself
si oneself; himself; herself; itself;
   themselves; each other
stesso/stessa: lo stesso/la stessa
   the same one
   gli stessi/le stesse the same ones
suo/sua/suoi/sue: il suo/la sua/
   i suoi/le sue his; hers; yours
tanti/tante many; so many

tanto/tanta much, so much
te you; to you
ti you; to you; yourself
troppi/troppe too many
troppo/troppa too much
tu you
tuo/tua/tuoi/tue: il tuo/la tua/
   i tuoi/le tue yours
tutti everybody
tutto everything
uno/una a, an; one
ve to you
vi you; to you; yourselves; each other
voi you
vostro/vostra/vostri/vostre:
   il vostro/la vostra/i vostri/le
   vostre yours

CONJUNCTIONS

> **What is a conjunction?**
> A **conjunction** is a word such as *and*, *but*, *or*, *so*, *if* and *because*, that links two words or phrases of a similar type, or two parts of a sentence, for example, *Diane <u>and</u> I have been friends for years; I left <u>because</u> I was bored*.

a meno che unless
affinché so that
anche too; even
ancora still; even
anzi in fact
anziché rather than; instead of
appena as soon as
benché although
che that; than
come how; as
comunque however
così: così ... che so ... that ...
  così ... come as ... as
dopo after
dunque so; well
e(d) and; but
eppure and yet
finché until; as long as
infatti in fact
ma but; however; nevertheless
mentre while

né: né... né... neither... nor...
nonostante even though
o or
  o... o... either... or...
oppure or
perché because; so that
perciò so
però but
per quanto however
pertanto therefore
poiché since
prima di before
purché as long as
pure too; even though
quando when
  da quando since
quindi so
se if; whether
sebbene even though
sia... che... both... and...
siccome since

ADJECTIVES

> **What is an adjective?**
> An **adjective** is a 'describing' word that tells you more about a person
> or thing, such as their appearance, colour, size or other qualities, for
> example, *pretty*, *blue*, *big*.

abbondante big
abile skilful
abituato(a): abituato a used to
acceso(a) on; burning; lit
accogliente pleasant; welcoming
accurato(a) detailed
acido(a) acid; sour
acuto(a) high; sharp; acute
adatto(a) right (for); suitable
addormentato(a) sleeping; asleep
aderente tight
affascinante very attractive
affaticato(a) tired
affettuoso(a) affectionate
affidabile reliable
affilato(a) sharp
affollato(a) crowded
afoso(a) muggy
aggiornato(a) up-to-date
agitato(a) nervous
allegro(a) cheerful
allucinante awful
alternativo(a) alternative
alto(a) high; tall; loud; deep
altro(a) other
amaro(a) bitter
ambedue both
amichevole friendly
ammalato(a) ill
ammobiliato(a) furnished
ampio(a) spacious; loose

analcolico(a) soft
anonimo(a) anonymous
antipatico(a) unpleasant
antiquato(a) old-fashioned
anziano(a) old
aperto(a) open
appuntito(a) sharp
armato(a) armed
arrabbiato(a) angry
arredato(a) furnished
arrugginito(a) rusty
asciutto(a) dry
aspro(a) sour
assente absent
assetato(a) thirsty
assortito(a) assorted
assurdo(a) ridiculous
astemio(a) teetotal
astratto(a) abstract
astuto(a) cunning
attento(a) careful
attillato(a) tight
attivo(a) active
attrezzato(a) equipped
attuale present; current
avaro(a) mean; stingy
bagnato(a) wet
basso(a) low; short; shallow
beato(a) blessed; lucky
bello(a) lovely; good-looking
benvenuto(a) welcome

biondo(a) blond
bollente boiling
bravo(a) good; clever
breve short
brusco(a) abrupt
brutto(a) ugly; bad
buffo(a) funny
buio(a) dark
buono(a) good
caldo(a) hot; warm
calmo(a) calm
capace able
capriccioso(a) naughty
carino(a) nice; nice-looking
caro(a) dear; expensive
cattivo(a) bad; nasty
celebre famous
certo(a) sure; certain
  certi(e) some
chiaro(a) clear; light; fair
chiuso(a) closed; locked
cieco(a) blind
colpevole guilty
colto(a) well-educated
comodo(a) comfortable
completo(a) complete; full
comprensivo(a) understanding
compreso(a) inclusive
comune common
congelato(a) frozen
conosciuto(a) well-known
contento(a) happy; glad
continuo(a) constant; nonstop
contrario(a) opposite
conveniente cheap
coperto(a) indoor; covered;
  overcast
corto(a) short
costoso(a) expensive

cotto(a) cooked
crespo(a) frizzy
cretino(a) stupid
croccante crisp; crusty
crudele cruel
crudo(a) raw
dannoso(a) harmful
debole weak
deluso(a) disappointed
denso(a) dense; thick
deprimente depressing
destro(a) right
determinato(a) certain;
  determined
difettoso(a) faulty
difficile difficult
diffidente suspicious
diffuso(a) common
diligente hard-working
dimagrante slimming
diretto(a) direct; through
diritto(a) straight
disabitato(a) uninhabited
disastroso(a) disastrous
discreto(a) reasonable; discreet
disgustoso(a) disgusting
disinvolto(a) relaxed
disonesto(a) dishonest
disordinato(a) untidy
dispari odd
disperato(a) desperate
dispettoso(a) spiteful
disponibile available
dissetante refreshing; thirst-
  quenching
distinto(a) distinguished; distinct
distratto(a) absent-minded
disubbidiente disobedient
diversi(e) several

diverso(a) different
divertente funny
dolce sweet
doloroso(a) painful; sad
doppio(a) double
dotato(a) gifted
drammatico(a) dramatic
duro(a) hard
eccellente excellent
eccezionale really good
eccitato(a) excited; aroused
ecologico(a) ecological
economico(a) inexpensive; economic
educato(a) polite
efficace effective
efficiente efficient
egoista selfish
elasticizzato(a) stretch
elementare basic; elementary; primary
elettrico(a) electric
emotivo(a) emotional
emozionante exciting
emozionato(a) moved; emotional
enorme huge
entrambi both
entusiasta enthusiastic; delighted
ereditario(a) hereditary
esatto(a) exact
esaurito(a) sold out; run down
esausto(a) exhausted
esclusivo(a) exclusive
escluso(a) except
esigente demanding
esotico(a) exotic
esplicito(a) explicit
esteriore exterior
esterno(a) outside

estero(a) foreign
estivo(a) summer
estremo(a) extreme
estroverso(a) outgoing
evidente obvious
facile easy
facoltativo(a) optional
falso(a) false; forged; fake
familiare familiar
famoso(a) famous
fantastico(a) great
fastidioso(a) annoying
faticoso(a) tiring
favoloso(a) fabulous
fedele faithful
felice happy
femminile feminine
feriale: giorno feriale week day
fermo(a) still; stopped
festivo: giorno festivo Sunday; holiday
fiero(a) proud
fine thin; fine; refined
finto(a) false; artificial; imitation
fisico(a) physical
fisso(a) fixed; permanent; regular
flessibile flexible
fondo(a) deep
forte strong; loud
fortunato(a) lucky
freddo(a) cold
frequentato(a) popular
frequente frequent
fresco(a) fresh; cool
fritto(a) fried
frizzante sparkling
furbo(a) clever
furibondo(a) furious
gassato(a) fizzy

gelato(a) frozen
gelido(a) icy
geloso(a) jealous
generoso(a) generous
geniale brilliant
gentile nice; kind
ghiacciato(a) frozen
gigante giant
giornaliero(a) daily
giovane young
giusto(a) right
goffo(a) clumsy
gonfio(a) swollen
grande big; great; grown-up
grasso(a) fat
gratuito(a) free
grave serious
grazioso(a) charming
grosso(a) big; large
guasto(a) not working
gustoso(a) tasty
handicappato(a) disabled
ideale ideal
identico(a) identical
idiota stupid
idratante moisturizing
imbarazzante awkward
imbarazzato(a) embarrassed
imbattibile unbeatable
imbottito(a) filled
imbranato(a) awkward; clumsy
immaturo(a) immature
immenso(a) huge
immobile motionless
impacciato(a) awkward
impanato(a) in breadcrumbs
impegnativo(a) demanding
impegnato(a) busy
impermeabile waterproof

impressionante terrible
imprevedibile unpredictable
imprevisto(a) unexpected
improvviso(a) sudden
inaffidabile unreliable
inaspettato(a) unexpected
incantevole lovely
incerto(a) uncertain
incinta pregnant
incluso(a) included
incollato(a) glued
incosciente unconscious; reckless
incustodito(a) unattended
indaffarato(a) busy
indimenticabile unforgettable
indipendente independent
indiretto(a) indirect
indispensabile essential
individuale personal
inesperto(a) inexperienced
infantile childish
infedele unfaithful
infelice unhappy
infinito(a) endless
infortunato(a) injured
infreddolito(a) cold
ingenuo(a) naïve
ingiusto(a) unfair
ingombrante cumbersome
innamorato(a) in love
insicuro(a) insecure
insolito(a) unusual
insopportabile unbearable
integrale wholemeal
internazionale international
interno(a) inside
intero(a) whole
intraprendente enterprising
inutile useless

invadente interfering
invalido(a) disabled
invernale winter
inverso(a) opposite
invidioso(a) jealous
istruito(a) well-educated
largo(a) wide
lavorativo(a) working
leale loyal
leggero(a) light
lento(a) slow
lesso(a) boiled
libero(a) free
limpido(a) clear
liquido(a) liquid
liscio(a) smooth; straight
logico(a) logical
logoro(a) threadbare
lontano(a) distant; far off
loro their
lucido(a) shiny; lucid
luminoso(a) bright; luminous
lunatico(a) temperamental
lungo(a) long
lussuoso(a) luxury
maggiore bigger; older
maggiorenne of age
magico(a) magic
magnetico(a) magnetic
magnifico(a) wonderful
magro(a) thin; low-fat
maiuscolo(a) capital
malato(a) ill, sick
maldestro(a) clumsy
maledetto(a) damn
maleducato(a) rude
malinconico(a) sad
malizioso(a) mischievous
malvagio(a) wicked

mancino(a) left-handed
manuale manual
marcio(a) rotten
maschile male; masculine
maschio(a) male
massimo(a) maximum
materno(a) maternal
matrimoniale matrimonial; double
matto(a) mad
maturo(a) ripe; mature
medesimo(a) same
medico(a) medical
medio(a) average
mensile monthly
meraviglioso(a) wonderful
meridionale southern
mezzo(a) half
migliore better
miliardario(a) billionaire
minimo(a) minimum; minimal
minore less; younger; smaller
minorenne under age
mio(a) my
miope short-sighted
misterioso(a) mysterious
misto(a) mixed
moderno(a) modern
modesto(a) modest
molle soft
molto(a) a lot of; much
  molti(e) many
mondiale world
morbido(a) soft
mortale fatal
morto(a) dead
mosso(a) rough; wavy; blurred
muto(a) dumb; silent
nasale nasal
nascosto(a) hidden

natalizio(a) Christmas
naturale natural; still
nauseante disgusting
necessario(a) necessary
nervoso(a) irritable
nessuno(a) no
netto(a) clear
neutro(a) neutral; neuter
nobile aristocratic
nocivo(a) harmful
noioso(a) boring
nostro(a) our
noto(a) well-known
notturno(a) night
nubile unmarried
nudo(a) naked
numeroso(a) numerous
nuovo(a) new
nutriente nourishing
nuvoloso(a) cloudy
obbediente obedient
obbligatorio(a) compulsory
obiettivo(a) objective
obliquo(a) oblique
occidentale western
occupato(a) occupied
odioso(a) hateful
offeso(a) offended
ogni every
onesto(a) honest
opportuno(a) right
ordinale ordinal
ordinato(a) tidy
orgoglioso(a) proud
orientale eastern
orizzontale horizontal
orrendo(a) awful
osceno(a) obscene
oscuro(a) unclear

ostile hostile
ostinato(a) stubborn
ottimista optimistic
ottimo(a) excellent
ovvio(a) obvious
pacifico(a) peaceful
pallido(a) pale
paralizzato(a) paralyzed
parecchi(e) quite a lot of
pari even
parziale partial
passato(a) last
passivo(a) passive
pauroso(a) awful
pazzo(a) crazy
pedonale pedestrian
peggiore worse
pelato(a) bald
peloso(a) hairy
pensieroso(a) thoughtful
penultimo(a) second from last
perfetto(a) perfect
pericoloso(a) dangerous
permaloso(a) touchy
permanente permanent
perplesso(a) puzzled
perso(a) lost
personale personal
perverso(a) perverse
pesante heavy
pessimista pessimistic
pessimo(a) very bad
piacevole pleasant
piatto(a) flat
piccante hot; spicy
piccolo(a) small; little; young
pieghevole folding
pieno(a) full
pignolo(a) fastidious

pigro(a) lazy
pittoresco(a) picturesque
poco(a) little
  pochi(e) few
popolare popular
portatile portable
potente powerful
povero(a) poor; unfortunate
pratico(a) practical
precipitoso(a) rash
preciso(a) precise
preferito(a) favourite
preoccupato(a) worried
presbite long-sighted
presuntuoso(a) conceited
prezioso(a) precious
primo(a) first
principale main
privato(a) private
profondo(a) deep
profumato(a) fragrant
pronto(a) ready
prossimo(a) next
provvisorio(a) provisional;
  temporary
prudente careful
pubblico(a) public
pudico(a) modest; demure
pulito(a) clean
puzzolente stinking
quadrato(a) square
qualche some
qual(e) which; what
qualsiasi any
quanto(a) how much
  quante(i) how many
quello(a) that
  quelli(e) those
questo(a) this

questi(e) these
quotidiano(a) daily
radicale radical
raffinato(a) sophisticated
ragionevole sensible; reasonable
randagio(a) stray
rapido(a) quick
raro(a) rare
rauco(a) hoarse
reale true
recente recent
redditizio(a) profitable
regionale regional
regolare regular
resistente strong
responsabile responsible
rettangolare rectangular
ricamato(a) embroidered
ricaricabile rechargeable
riccio(a) curly
ricco(a) rich
riconoscente grateful
ricoperto(a) covered
ridicolo(a) funny
ridotto(a) reduced
riflessivo(a) reflexive
rigido(a) stiff
ripido(a) steep
ripieno(a) stuffed
rischioso(a) risky
riservato(a) reserved
risolto(a) solved
robusto(a) strong
roco(a) hoarse
rotondo(a) round
rotto(a) broken
rumoroso(a) noisy
ruvido(a) rough
sacro(a) sacred

saggio(a) wise
salato(a) salty
sano(a) healthy; sane
santo(a) holy
saporito(a) tasty
sbadato(a) careless
sbagliato(a) wrong
sbiadito(a) faded
sbronzo(a) drunk
scadente poor-quality
scalzo(a) barefoot
scarico(a) not loaded; flat
scarso(a) scarce
scemo(a) stupid
schifoso(a) disgusting
schizzinoso(a) fussy
sciocco(a) silly
scivoloso(a) slippery
scolastico(a) school
scollato(a) low-cut
scolorito(a) faded
scomodo(a) uncomfortable
sconosciuto(a) unknown
scontento(a) unhappy
sconvolto(a) upset
scoperto(a) bare; uncovered
scorretto(a) incorrect
scorrevole flowing; fluent
scorso(a) last
scortese rude; impolite
scosso(a) shaken
scotto(a) overcooked
scremato(a) skimmed
scuro(a) dark
seccato(a) annoyed
secco(a) dry
secondo(a) second
segreto(a) secret
seguente following

selvaggio(a) wild
selvatico(a) wild
semplice simple
sensibile sensitive
sensuale sensual
sentimentale sentimental
separato(a) separate; separated
serale evening
sereno(a) calm
serio(a) serious
sessuale sexual
settentrionale northern
settimanale weekly
severo(a) strict; severe
sfacciato(a) cheeky
sfinito(a) exhausted
sfocato(a) out of focus
sfortunato(a) unlucky
sgarbato(a) rude
sgonfio(a) flat
sgradevole unpleasant
sgraziato(a) clumsy
sicuro(a) safe
sieronegativo(a) HIV-negative
sieropositivo(a) HIV-positive
silenzioso(a) quiet
simile similar
simpatico(a) nice
sincero(a) honest
sinistro(a) left
sintetico(a) synthetic
sleale disloyal
snello(a) slim
snervante stressful
sobrio(a) sober
sociale social
socievole sociable
soddisfatto(a) pleased
soffice soft

soffocante stifling
sofisticato(a) sophisticated
solare solar; sun
solido(a) solid
solitario(a) lonely
solito(a) usual
solo(a) alone
sonoro(a) loud
soprannaturale supernatural
sordo(a) deaf
sordomuto(a) deaf-and-dumb
sorprendente surprising
sorpreso(a) surprised
sorridente smiling
sospettoso(a) suspicious
sotterraneo(a) underground
sottile thin
sottinteso(a) understood
sovraccarico(a) overloaded
spaesato(a) lost
spaventoso(a) terrible
spazioso(a) spacious
speciale special
spensierato(a) carefree
spento(a) off
spesso(a) thick
spettinato(a) uncombed
spezzato(a) broken
spiacevole unpleasant
spiritoso(a) witty
spontaneo(a) spontaneous
sporco(a) dirty
sposato(a) married
squallido(a) dingy
squilibrato(a) deranged
squisito(a) delicious
stabile stable
stagionato(a) seasoned
stanco(a) tired

stonato(a) tone-deaf
stordito(a) stunned
storico(a) historical; memorable
storto(a) crooked
stradale road
straniero(a) foreign
strano(a) strange
straordinario(a) extraordinary
stravagante eccentric
stravolto(a) distraught
stressante stressful
stressato(a) stressed
stretto(a) narrow; tight
stridulo(a) shrill
studioso(a) studious
stufo(a) fed up
stupendo(a) wonderful
subacqueo(a) underwater
successivo(a) following
sudato(a) sweaty
suo(a) his; her; your
superbo(a) proud; haughty
superfluo(a) superfluous
superiore upper; secondary
supplementare extra
surgelato(a) frozen
svantaggiato(a) disadvantaged
sveglio(a) awake
svelto(a) quick
tagliente sharp
tale such
tanto(a) a lot of
tascabile pocket-sized
tenero(a) tender
teso(a) tense
testardo(a) stubborn
tiepido(a) lukewarm
tipico(a) typical; traditional
tirchio(a) mean

tondo(a) round
tranquillo(a) quiet
triste sad
troppi(e) too many
troppo(a) too much
tuo(a) your
turbato(a) upset
tutto(a) all
ubriaco(a) drunk
ufficiale official
uguale equal
ultimo(a) last; latest
umano(a) human
umido(a) damp
umile humble
unico(a) only
unto(a) greasy
urgente urgent
usato(a) second-hand
utile useful

valido(a) valid
vario(a) varied; various
vecchio(a) old
vegetale vegetable
vegetariano(a) vegetarian
velenoso(a) poisonous
veloce fast
vergognoso(a) terrible
vero(a) true; real; genuine
vicino(a) near; close by
vietato(a) forbidden
vivace lively; bright
vivo(a) alive; live
viziato(a) spoilt
vostro(a) your
vuoto(a) empty
zitto(a) quiet
zoppo(a) lame
zuccherato(a) sweetened
zuppo(a) soaked; drenched

ADVERBS AND PREPOSITIONS

> **What is an adverb?**
> An **adverb** is a word usually used with verbs, adjectives or other adverbs that gives more information about when, how, where or in what cirumstances something happens, or to what degree something is true, for example, *quickly, happily, now, extremely, very*.

> **What is a preposition?**
> A **preposition** is a word such as *at, for, with, into* or *from*, which is usually followed by a noun, pronoun, or, in English, a word ending in *-ing*. Prepositions show how people or things relate to the rest of the sentence, for example, *She's at home; a tool for cutting grass; It's from David*.

a at; in; to
abbastanza quite; enough
accanto near
addirittura even
adesso now
affatto at all
allora then; so
almeno at least
altrettanto equally
altrimenti or; another way
ancora still; more; again
appena just; only just
apposta on purpose; specially
assai very; much
assieme together
attorno round
attraverso through
attualmente at the moment
avanti forward
  in avanti forward
bene well
ci there; here
cioè that is
circa about

come how; like; as
comunque anyway
con with
continuamente nonstop
contro against
correntemente fluently
così so; like this
da from; to; since
daccapo from the beginning
dappertutto everywhere
davanti at the front; in front of; opposite
davvero really
dentro in; inside
di of; by
dietro behind
diritto straight on
domani tomorrow
dopo after; later; then
dopodomani the day after tomorrow
doppio double
dove where
dovunque wherever; everywhere

durante during
eccetto except
ecco here
entro by
  entro domani by tomorrow
esattamente exactly
essenzialmente essentially
estremamente extremely
evidentemente obviously
fa ago
finalmente at last
fino a until; as far as
finora yet; so far
forse maybe
forte fast; hard; loud
fra between; among; in
  fra poco soon
fuori outside; out
già already
giù down
giusto just
gratis free
gravemente seriously
ieri yesterday
improvvisamente suddenly;
  unexpectedly
in in; to; into; by
incirca: all'incirca about
indietro back
infine finally
infuori out
innanzitutto first of all
inoltre besides
insieme together
insomma well
intanto for now; but
intorno round
inutilmente unnecessarily
invece but

invece di instead of
là (over) there
laggiù down there; over there
lassù up there
lentamente slowly
lì there
liscio smoothly
lontano far
  da lontano from a distance
lungo along
mai never
  quasi mai hardly ever
  mai più never again
malapena: a malapena hardly
male badly
malgrado in spite of
mediante by means of
meglio better
meno less; fewer; minus; except
  a meno che unless
  di meno less
  più o meno more or less
  meno… di less… than
molto a lot; much; very
naturalmente of course
neanche not even; neither
  non … neanche not even…
nemmeno not even; neither
  non … nemmeno not even…
no no; not
non not
nonostante in spite of
nuovamente again
oggi today
oggigiorno nowadays
oltre over
  oltre a apart from
ora now; per ora for now
ormai by now

supplementary vocabulary

ovunque wherever; everywhere
peggio worse
per for; through; by; to
perché why
perfettamente perfectly
perfino even
persino even
piano slowly; quietly
  pian piano little by little
più more
  più di more than
  di più more
  in più more
  più o meno more or less
  mai più never again
piuttosto rather
po': un po' a little
poco not much
  tra poco soon
poi then; later
  prima o poi sooner or later
praticamente practically
precisamente precisely
pressappoco about
presto soon; early
prima before; earlier
  prima possibile as soon as
  possible
principalmente mainly
proprio just; really
purtroppo unfortunately
qua (over) here
quaggiù down here
quando when
quanto how much; how long
quasi nearly; hardly
  quasi mai hardly ever
quassù up here
qui here

quindi then
rapidamente quickly
raramente rarely
realmente really
recentemente recently
salvo except
secondo according to
sempre always; still
  per sempre forever
  sempre meno less and less
senza without
sì yes
solamente only
solo only
soltanto only
sopra over; above; on top of
  di sopra upstairs
soprattutto mainly; especially
sotto under; below
sottosopra upside down
sottoterra underground
sottovoce in a low voice; softly
specialmente especially
spesso often
stamattina this morning
stanotte tonight; last night
stasera this evening
stavolta this time
su on; up; about
subito immediately
talmente so much; so
tanto so; so much
tardi late
tra between; among; in
tranne except
troppo too
tuttavia but
ultimamente lately
veramente really; actually

verso towards; about *(of time)*
vi there
via away

viceversa vice versa
volentieri willingly

SOME EXTRA NOUNS

> **What is a noun?**
> A noun is a naming word for a living being, a thing, or an idea, for
> example, *woman*, *Andrew*, *desk*, *happiness*.

l' abbazia abbey
l' abbigliamento clothes
l' abbreviazione f abbreviation
l' abilità skill
l' abitante m/f inhabitant
l' abitudine f habit
l' aborto abortion; miscarriage
l' accento accent; stress
l' accesso access
l' accordo agreement; chord
l' addestramento training
l' addizione f sum
l' affermazione f statement
l' affetto affection
l' aggettivo adjective
l' aiuto help
l' alfabeto alphabet
l' alimentazione f diet
l' alito breath
l' allarme m alarm
l' allenamento training
l' allenatore m coach
l' allenatrice f coach
l' alloggio accommodation
l' allusione f hint
l' alternativa alternative
l' ambiente m environment
l' ambizione f ambition
l' amicizia friendship
l' ammirazione f admiration
l' amore m love
l' analfabeta m/f illiterate
l' analgesico painkiller

l' anestesia anaesthesia
l' angelo angel
l' angolo corner; angle
l' anima soul
l' anticipo advance
   essere in anticipo to be early
l' antifurto (pl inv) burglar alarm; car
   alarm
l' apertura opening
l' apostrofo apostrophe
l' apparecchio device; brace
l' appoggio support
l' apprendimento learning
l' argomento subject
l' ascella armpit
l' aspetto appearance
l' assenza absence
l' assicurazione f insurance
l' associazione f association
l' astuccio case
l' atmosfera atmosphere
l' atrio entrance; concourse
l' attaccapanni m (pl inv) hook
l' atteggiamento attitude
l' attentato attack
l' attenzione f attention
l' attesa wait
l' attimo minute
l' attività (pl inv) activity
l' attualità current affairs
l' audizione f audition
l' aumento increase
l' autografo autograph

l' autorità *(pl inv)* authority
l' avorio ivory
l' avvenimento event
l' avventura adventure; affair
l' azione *f* action; deed; share
la bacinella bowl
la badante care worker
la bancarella stall
la banconota note
la bandiera flag
la bara coffin
la baracca *(pl -che)* hut
il barattolo jar; tin; pot
il barboncino poodle
il barbone tramp
la barella stretcher
la barzelletta joke
la battuta jok
il becco *(pl -chi)* beak
la beneficenza charity
la bevanda drink
la biancheria sheets and towels;
  underwear
la bilancia *(pl -ce)* scales
il bisogno need
il bivio junction
la bolletta bill
il bollitore kettle
la bombola cylinder
il bordo edge; border
  a bordo on board
il borotalco talcum powder
la briciola crumb
il brillante diamond
il brindisi toast
la buccia *(pl -ce)* peel; rind
la bugia lie
la bugiarda liar
il bugiardo liar

il buonumore: essere di
  buonumore to be in a good mood
il burattino puppet
la bussola compass
la busta envelope
la bustarella bribe
la caccia hunting
il cacciatore hunter
il cadavere dead body
la caduta fall
la calamita magnet
il calcagno heel
la calligrafia handwriting
la calma calm
il calo drop
il camino chimney
il cammello camel
il campanile bell tower
il campionato championship
il cancello gate
la cannuccia *(pl -ce)* drinking straw
il capitolo chapter
il capriccio whim
la capriola somersault
la caratteristica *(pl -che)* feature
il carcere prison
la carestia famine
la cascata waterfall
la caserma barracks
il castigo *(pl -ghi)* punishment
il catalogo *(pl -ghi)* catalogue
il catrame tar
la causa cause
la cenere ash
il cerchietto hairband
il cerchio circle
il cespuglio bush
la cicatrice scar
il cimitero graveyard

la **circostanza** circumstance
il **citofono** entry phone; intercom
il **ciuccio** dummy
la **civiltà** (pl inv) civilization
la **classifica** (pl -che) results; charts;
  league table
il **codino** ponytail
il **collasso** collapse
il **collegamento** link
la **colpa** fault; blame
il/la **colpevole** culprit
il **colpo** blow; shot; raid
la **combinazione** combination;
  coincidence
la **comitiva** group
la **commozione** emotion
il/la **complice** accomplice
la **complicità** collusion
il/la **concorrente** competitor;
  contestant
la **condizione** condition
la **confezione** packet
la **consegna** delivery
la **conseguenza** consequence
il **consiglio** advice
la **consolazione** consolation
i **contanti** cash
il **contenitore** container
il **contenuto** contents
il **continente** continent; mainland
il **conto** bill; account; calculation
  per conto mio in my opinion; on
  my own
il **contrabbando** smuggling
il **contratto** contract
la **conversazione** conversation
il **coro** choir
la **correzione** correction
la **costruzione** building

il **crimine** crime
la **crisi** (pl inv) crisis; fit
la **croce** cross
la **crociera** cruise
il **cronometro** stopwatch
il **culturismo** body-building
la **cupola** dome
la **custodia** case
il **danno** damage
la **dattilografia** typing
il **debito** debt
la **debolezza** weakness
la **decisione** decision
il **delitto** crime
la **delusione** disappointment
la **descrizione** description
la **destinazione** destination
il **dialetto** dialect
la **dichiarazione** declaration;
  statement
la **didascalia** caption; subtitle
il **difetto** fault
la **differenza** difference
la **diga** (pl -ghe) dam; breakwater
il **digiuno** fasting
il/la **dipendente** employee
il **dipinto** painting
la **disapprovazione** disapproval
la **discesa** slope; descent
la **disciplina** discipline
il **discorso** speech
il **disordine** mess
il **disprezzo** contempt
la **distruzione** destruction
la **dormigliona** sleepyhead
il **dormiglione** sleepyhead
la **dozzina** dozen
l' **eccezione** f exception
l' **eclisse** f eclipse

l' **entusiasmo** enthusiasm
l' **epoca** (*pl* -che) era
l' **equitazione** f riding
l' **equivoco** misunderstanding
l' **eredità** (*pl inv*) inheritance
l' **esclamazione** f exclamation
l' **esempio** example
l' **esercito** army
l' **esilio** exile
l' **esperimento** experiment
l' **espressione** f expression
l' **estinzione** f extinction
l' **etichetta** label
la **faccenda** matter
il **fallimento** bankruptcy; failure
la **fantascienza** science fiction
la **fantasia** imagination; pattern
il **fascino** charm
la **fase** phase
la **fata** fairy
la **fatica** (*pl* -che) effort
il **fatto** fact
la **felicità** happiness
la **ferita** injury; wound
la **fessura** crack; slot
il **fiato** breath; stamina
il **fidanzamento** engagement
la **fiducia** trust
la **filastrocca** (*pl* -che) nursery
   rhyme
il **filo** thread; yarn; wire
la **finanza** finance
il **fine** end
   fine settimana weekend
la **fine** end
   alla fine in the end
la **firma** signature
il **fischio** whistle
la **fodera** lining; cover

la **fogna** sewer
la **folla** crowd
la **follia** madness
la **fortuna** luck; fortune
la **fototessera** passport-size photo
la **frattura** fracture
la **freccia** (*pl* -ce) arrow; indicator
la **frusta** whip
il **fumetto** comic strip; comic
la **funivia** cablecar
la **funzione** function
la **gabbia** cage
la **galera** prison
il **gambo** stem
il **gancio** hook
la **gara** competition
la **gelosia** jealousy
la **generazione** generation
il **genere** kind; gender
il **gesso** chalk; plaster
la **gestione** management
il **gettone** token
la **giornata** day
la **giostra** roundabout
   le **giostre** funfair
la **gita** trip
il **giudizio** opinion
la **giustificazione** excuse
la **goccia** (*pl* -ce) drop
il **gonfiore** swelling
il **granello** grain; speck
la **gravidanza** pregnancy
la **gru** (*pl inv*) crane
la **gruccia** (*pl* -ce) crutch; coat
   hanger
il **guasto** failure
la **guerra** war
il **guinzaglio** dog lead
l' **identità** (*pl inv*) identity

l' idolo idol
l' illusione f illusion
l' imballaggio packing
l' immaginazione f imagination
l' impegno engagement;
  commitment
l' impianto system
l' importo amount
l' imposta shutter; tax
l' imprenditore m entrepreneur
l' imprenditrice f entrepreneur
l' impresa business
l' incertezza uncertainty
l' incubo nightmare
l' incursione f raid
l' indagine f investigation
l' indovinello riddle
l' inesperienza inexperience
l' inferno hell
l' infezione f infection
l' ingrediente m ingredient
l' iniezione f injection
l' inizio beginning
l' insegnamento teaching
l' intimità privacy
l' inviata correspondent
l' inviato correspondent
l' invidia envy
l' iscrizione f registration
il labbro lip
la lama blade
il lampadario chandelier
il lampo flash of lightning
la larghezza width
la lastra slab; sheet; X-ray
il lato side; aspect
la letteratura literature
il lievito yeast
la lineetta hyphen; dash

la lisca (pl -che) fishbone
il livido bruise
la lotta struggle
il lucchetto padlock
la lunghezza length
il luogo (pl -ghi) place
la macchia stain
la madrelingua mother tongue
la maga (pl -ghe) sorceress
il magazzino warehouse
la maggioranza majority
il/la maggiore the older; the oldest
la magia magic
il male evil
la maledizione curse
la maleducazione bad manners
la malinconia melancholy
il malinteso misunderstanding
la mancanza lack
la manciata handful
le manette handcuffs
la manifestazione demonstration;
  event
la maniglia handle
la maratona marathon
la marca (pl -che) make; brand
il mazzo bunch; pack
la media average
il/la mendicante beggar
la mensola shelf
la mente mind
la menzogna lie
la merce goods
il mestiere job
la metà (pl inv) half
il miglioramento improvement
la minaccia (pl -ce) threat
la minoranza minority
il miracolo miracle

la miseria poverty
il mito myth
la mitologia mythology
il/la mittente sender
la modifica (*pl* -che) modification;
  alteration
il modulo form
la morte death
la mostra exhibition
il motivo reason
la muffa mould
la multa fine
il mutuo mortgage
il nascondiglio hiding place
il nastro ribbon; tape
la nazione nation
il neo mole
la neonata newborn baby
il neonato newborn baby
la ninnananna lullaby
il nodo knot; tangle
la noia boredom
la norma norm
la nostalgia homesickness
le nozze wedding
l' obbligo (*pl* -ghi) obligation
l' obiettivo lens; aim
l' obiezione *f* objection
l' occasione *f* opportunity; occasion;
  bargain
l' odio hatred
l' odore *m* smell
l' offesa insult
l' omaggio gift
l' ombelico (*pl* -chi) navel
l' omicidio murder
l' onestà honesty
l' opinione *f* opinion
l' opuscolo booklet

l' organizzazione *f* organization
l' origine *f* origin
l' orizzonte *m* horizon
l' orlo edge; brink; brim; hem
l' orma track; footprint
l' ormone *m* hormone
l' ortografia spelling
l' osservazione *f* observation;
  remark
l' ossigeno oxygen
l' ostacolo difficulty; hurdle
l' ostaggio hostage
l' ottimismo optimism
l' otturazione *f* filling
il paesaggio landscape
la palestra gym
la palude marsh
il pannello panel
il panno cloth
il paracadute (*pl inv*) parachute
il paradiso heaven
il paragrafo paragraph
il pareggio draw
la parentesi (*pl inv*) bracket
il parere *m* opinion
la parolaccia (*pl* -ce) swearword
il particolare detail
il/la passante passer-by
il passatempo pastime
il passato past
la passione passion
il pasto meal
il patto pact
la pazza madman
il pazzo madman
il peccato shame; sin
il pedaggio toll
il pedone pedestrian
il/la pendolare commuter

il **pennello** paintbrush
il **pensiero** thought; worry
la **pensionata** pensioner
il **pensionato** pensioner
la **percentuale** percentage
il **percorso** route
la **perdita** loss; waste
la **permanenza** stay
il **personaggio** character
il **personale** staff
la **personalità** (pl inv) personality
la **peste** plague; pest
la **pettinatura** hairstyle
il **pettine** comb
il **pianerottolo** landing
il **pianeta** planet
il **piatto** dish; plate; **i piatti** the
   cymbals
la **piega** (pl -ghe) fold; pleat; crease
la **pietà** pity
la **pigrizia** laziness
la **pinacoteca** (pl -che) art gallery
il **pisolino** nap
la **pistola** gun
la **piuma** feather
il **pizzico** (pl -chi) pinch
il **podio** podium
la **polemica** (pl -che) controversy
il **polline** pollen
la **pomata** ointment
la **popolazione** population
il **popolo** people
il **portatelefonino** mobile phone
   case
il/la **portavoce** (pl inv)
   spokesperson
il **portone** main entrance
la **porzione** portion
la **posa** exposure; pose

le **posate** cutlery
la **posizione** position
la **possibilità** (pl inv) possibility;
   opportunity
la **potenza** power
il **potere** power
la **povertà** poverty
la **pozzanghera** puddle
la **precauzione** precaution
la **preda** prey
la **prefazione** preface
la **preferenza** preference
la **preghiera** prayer
il **pregio** good quality
il **pregiudizio** prejudice
il **prelievo** withdrawal
la **premiazione** prize-giving; award
   ceremony
la **preoccupazione** worry
i **preparativi** preparations
la **presa** grip
il **presepio** crib
il **preservativo** condom
la **pressione** pressure
il **prestito** loan
il **preventivo** estimate
il/la **principiante** beginner
il **principio** beginning; principle
la **probabilità** (pl inv) chance
il **problema** problem
la **profondità** depth
il **progetto** plan
il **progresso** progress
il **proiettile** bullet
la **prolunga** (pl -ghe) extension
il **pronome** pronoun
la **pronuncia** (pl -ce) pronunciation
il **proposito** intention
la **proposizione** clause

la proposta suggestion
la prospettiva prospect;
  perspective
la protezione protection
la provetta test tube
il provino screen test; trailer
la provocazione provocation
il provvedimento measure
il pubblico public; audience
la punizione punishment
la punta point; top; touch
  doppie punte split ends
la puntata episode; flying visit
la punteggiatura punctuation
il punteggio score
il punto point; stitch; full stop
la puntura injection; sting; bite
la puzza stink
il quadrifoglio four-leaf clover
la questione matter
la quota membership fee
il quotidiano daily paper
la raccolta collection
il raccolto harvest
il racconto short story
la radiazione radiation
la radice root
la ragione reason
il ramo branch; field
il rapimento kidnapping
la rapina robbery
il rapporto relationship; report
la rappresentazione
  representation; play
la rata instalment
la razza race; breed; sort
il razzismo racism
il reato crime
la reazione reaction

il rebus picture puzzle
la recensione review
il recipiente container
il reddito income
il regolamento rules
la reputazione reputation
il requisito requirement
la respirazione breathing
il respiro breath
la riabilitazione rehabilitation
il riassunto summary
il ricatto blackmail
il ricciolo curl
la ricerca (pl -che) search; research;
  project
la richiesta request
la ricompensa reward
la ricreazione recreation; break
il riferimento reference
il rifiuto refusal
la riflessione remark; thought
il riflesso reflection; reflex
il rimorso remorse
il rimpianto regret
il Rinascimento Renaissance
la ringhiera railing; banisters
il rinvio (pl -ii) postponement
il risparmio saving
il rispetto respect
la risposta answer
il ritornello refrain
il ritratto portrait
la rivelazione revelation
la rivincita rematch
la ruga (pl -ghe) wrinkle
la ruggine rust
la rugiada dew
il sacrificio sacrifice
la sagoma outline; shape

la salita climb; hill
il salvadanaio money box
lo sbadiglio yawn
lo sbaglio mistake
la sbarra bar
la scadenza expiry date; sell-by
   date; use-by date
lo scaffale bookcase
lo scatto click; spurt
la scelta choice
lo sceneggiato TV drama
lo scheletro skeleton
lo schema diagram
lo scherzo joke
la schiava slave
lo schiavo slave
la schiuma foam; lather
lo schizzo splash; sketch
la sciagura disaster
lo scioglilingua (pl inv) tongue-
   twister
la scommessa bet
la sconfitta defeat
lo sconto discount
lo scontrino receipt slip
lo scontro crash; clash
la scoperta discovery
lo scopo aim
lo scoppio explosion; bang
la scorciatoia short cut
la scottatura burn; sunburn
la scrittura writing
la scrivania desk
lo scudo shield
la scusa excuse
la seccatura nuisance; bother
la semifinale semifinal
la sensazione feeling
il senso sense; direction

il settore sector
la sezione section
la sfida challenge
lo sfondo background
la sfortuna bad luck
lo sforzo effort
lo sfruttamento exploitation
la sfumatura shade; tone
lo sgabello stool
lo sgabuzzino junk room
lo sguardo look
la siccità drought
la sicurezza safety
la sigla acronym
il significato meaning
il silenzio silence
la sillaba syllable
il simbolo symbol
il sinonimo synonym
il sintomo symptom
il sistema system; way
la sistemazione accommodation
la situazione situation
lo smacchiatore stain remover
la smagliatura ladder; stretch mark
la soddisfazione satisfaction
il soffio breath
il solitario game of patience
la solitudine loneliness
il sollievo relief
la soluzione solution
il sommario summary
la sonnambula sleepwalker
il sonnambulo sleepwalker
il sonnifero sleeping pill
il sonno sleep
il soprannome nickname
il sorso sip
la sorte fate

il/la sosia (*pl inv*) double
il sospetto suspicion
il sospiro sigh
il sostantivo noun
la sostituzione substitution
la sovvenzione subsidy
la spaccatura split
la spacciatrice drug dealer
lo spacciatore drug dealer
lo spacco (*pl* -chi) slit
lo spago (*pl* -ghi) string
la spallina shoulder strap
lo sparo shot
lo spavento fright
lo specchietto pocket mirror
la specialità (*pl inv*) speciality
la specie (*pl inv*) sort; species
la speculazione speculation
la speranza hope
lo spettatore viewer; spectator
  gli spettotori the audience
le spezie spices
la spia spy; light
gli spiccioli loose change
lo spiedino kebab; skewer
la spiegazione explanation
la spinta push
lo sportello door; window
lo spuntino snack
lo starnuto sneeze
la stenografia shorthand
la stilografica (*pl* -che) fountain pen
la stima respect
la strage massacre
lo straordinario overtime
lo strappo tear; lift
lo strato layer
la strega (*pl* -ghe) witch
lo strillo scream

la striscia (*pl* -sce) strip
lo striscione banner
la struttura structure
lo stupore amazement
lo stupro rape
il suggerimento suggestion
il suicidio suicide
la suoneria alarm; ringtone
il suono sound
la superficie surface
il/la superiore superior
la superstizione superstition
lo svantaggio disadvantage
il taglio cut
la tappa stop
la targa (*pl* -ghe) number plate
la targhetta nameplate; name tag
la tastiera keyboard
il tatuaggio tattoo
la teiera teapot
la tela cloth
il temperino penknife
la tentazione temptation
la teoria theory
il terreno land; ground
il territorio territory
il/la terrorista terrorist
il teschio skull
il tessuto fabric
il testamento will
il/la testimone witness
la tifosa supporter
il tifoso supporter
il tipo sort; type
la tomba grave
il tono tone
il torcicollo stiff neck
il tornante hairpin bend
il torneo tournament

il totocalcio the pools
la traccia (pl -ce) trace
la tradizione tradition
la traduzione translation
la trama plot
il tramonto sunset
il trapano drill
il trapianto transplant
il trasloco (pl -chi) removal
la trasmissione programme
il trattino hyphen
il tratto stretch
il trauma shock
la treccia (pl -ce) plait
il tribunale court
il triciclo tricycle
il trono throne
il truffatore swindler
il tumore tumour
il tuorlo yolk
il turbante turban
l'udito hearing
l'umore m mood
l'unificazione f unification
l'urlo scream
l'usanza custom
l'uso use; usage
l'ustione f burn
la valanga (pl -ghe) avalanche
la valvola valve
il valzer (pl inv) waltz
il vandalismo vandalism
il vangelo gospel
la varietà variety
il vasetto jar

il vassoio tray
la vedova widow
il vedovo widower
il veicolo vehicle
il veleno poison
la vergogna embarrassment
la vernice varnish; paint; patent leather
la verità (pl inv) truth
il vero truth
la vicenda event; story
il vincitore winner
la vincitrice winner
la virgola comma; point
le virgolette inverted commas
la vita life; waist
la vittima victim
la vittoria victory
il vizio bad habit; vice
il vocabolario dictionary
il volo flight
la volontà will
il volume volume
il voto mark; vote
il vuoto gap
il wafer (pl inv) wafer
il water (pl inv) toilet
il W.C. (pl inv) W.C.
la zingara gypsy
lo zingaro gypsy
la zitella spinster
lo zoccolo clog; hoof; skirting board
lo zodiaco zodiac

VERBS

> **What is a verb?**
> A **verb** is a 'doing' word which describes what someone or something
> does, what someone or something is, or what happens to them, for
> example, *be*, *sing*, *live*.

abbandonare to abandon; to give up

abbassare to lower

abbracciarsi to hug

abbronzarsi to get tanned

abitare to live

abituarsi: abituarsi a (fare) qc to get used to (doing) sth

accadere to happen

accamparsi to camp

accarezzare to stroke

accelerare to accelerate

accendere to light; to turn on

accettare to accept

accludere to enclose

accogliere to welcome

accomodarsi to sit down

accompagnare to take ... to

accontentare to please

  accontentarsi di to make do with

accorciare to shorten

accorgersi to notice; to realize

acquistare to buy

addormentarsi to go/fall to sleep

adottare to adopt

afferrare to grab; to catch

affettare to slice

affittare to rent

affogare to drown

affondare to sink

affrettarsi to hurry up

agganciare to hook; to hang up

aggiungere to add

aggiustare to mend; to straighten

aggredire to attack

agire to act

agitare to shake

  agitarsi to worry

aiutare to help

allacciare to fasten; to connect

allagare to flood

allargare to widen

allearsi to join forces

allegare to enclose

allenare to train

alloggiare to stay

allungare to lengthen

alzare to lift; to raise

  alzarsi to get up

amare to love

ammalarsi to get ill

ammazzare to kill

ammettere to admit

ammirare to admire

andare to go

  andarsene to leave

annaffiare to water

annegare to drown

annoiare to bore

  annoiarsi to get bored

annullare to cancel

annunciare to announce

apparire to appear

appartenere to belong

appendere to hang
appoggiare to put; to lean
approfittare: approfittare di qc to make the most of sth
aprire to open; to turn on
arrabbiarsi to get angry
arrampicarsi to climb
arrangiarsi to get by
arrestare to arrest
arrivare to arrive
arrossire to blush
asciugare to dry
ascoltare to listen to
aspettare to wait; to expect
assaggiare to taste
assicurare to insure; to assure
assistere to look after; to watch; to witness
assomigliare a to look like
assumere to take on
atterrare to land
attirare to attract; to appeal to
attraversare to cross; to go through
aumentare to go up
avanzare to be left over
avere to have
  avere fame to be hungry
  avere sete to be thirsty
  avere paura to be afraid
  avere sonno to be sleepy
avvelenare to poison
avvertire to warn
avvicinare to move closer
baciare to kiss
badare to pay attention; to mind
bagnare to get wet; to water
ballare to dance
bastare to be enough
battere to beat; to hit

bere to drink
bestemmiare to swear
bisbigliare to whisper
bisticciare to quarrel
brillare to shine
brontolare to moan
bruciare to burn
bucare to have a puncture
  bucarsi to be on heroin
bussare to knock
buttare to throw
  buttare via to throw away
cacciare to hunt
cadere to fall
calare to decrease; to drop
calcolare to work out
cambiare to change
  cambiarsi to get changed
camminare to walk
cancellare to cancel; to delete
cantare to sing
capire to understand
  capire male to misunderstand
capitare to happen
caricare to (up)load; to charge
cavalcare to ride
cenare to have dinner
cercare to look for; to look up; to try
chiacchierare to chat
chiamare to call; to phone
chiarire to clarify
chiedere to ask; to ask for
  chiedersi to wonder
chiudere to close; to turn off
  chiudere a chiave to lock
cogliere to pick
coinvolgere to involve
collegare to connect
colpire to hit

comandare to be in charge
combattere to fight
cominciare to start
compilare to fill in
comporre to dial; to compose
comportarsi to behave
comprare to buy
condire to dress; to season
condividere to share
confermare to confirm
confondere to mix up
  confondersi to get mixed up
connettere to connect
conoscere to know
  conoscersi to meet
consegnare to deliver
conservare to keep
consigliare to recommend; to advise
consumare to wear out; to use
contare to count
  contare su qn to count on sb
contenere to contain
continuare to carry on
controllare to check
  controllarsi to control oneself
convenire to be cheaper
convincere to convince
  convincere qn a fare qc to persuade sb to do sth
copiare to copy
coprire to cover
correggere to correct; to mark
correre to run
costare to cost
credere to believe; to think
crescere to grow
cucinare to cook
cucire to sew

curare to treat
danneggiare to damage
dare to give
  dare su to look onto
decidere to decide
  decidersi to decide
decollare to take off
deludere to disappoint
denunciare to report; to expose
derubare to rob
descrivere to describe
desiderare to want
detrarre to deduct
deviare to divert
dichiarare to declare; to state
digerire to digest
dimagrire to lose weight
dimenticare to forget
dimettersi to resign
diminuire to decrease; to reduce
dimostrare to demonstrate
dipingere to paint
dire to say
dirigere to manage
discutere to discuss; to argue
disdire to cancel
disegnare to draw; to design
disfare to undo
distendere to stretch
  distendersi to lie down; to relax
distrarre to distract
  distrarsi to take one's mind off things
distribuire to distribute
distruggere to destroy
disubbidire: disubbidire a qn to disobey sb
diventare to become
divertire to amuse

divertirsi to have a good time
divorziare to get divorced
domandare to ask
domandarsi to wonder
dondolarsi to rock; to swing
dormire to sleep
dovere to have to
dovere qc a qn to owe sb sth
durare to last
emozionare: emozionarsi to be moved; to be excited
entrare to enter
esagerare to exaggerate
esaurire to sell out; to run out of
eseguire to carry out; to perform
esercitare to practise; to train
esigere to demand
esporre to display; to exhibit
esportare to export
esprimere to express
essere to be
estrarre to extract
evadere to escape
evitare to avoid
fabbricare to make
fallire to go bankrupt; to fail
fare to make; to do
fasciare to bandage
ferire to injure; to wound
fermare to stop
festeggiare to celebrate
fidanzarsi to get engaged
fidarsi: fidarsi di qn to trust sb
fingere to pretend
finire to finish
firmare to sign
fischiare to whistle
fissare to fix; to stare at
fornire to supply

forzare to force
fraintendere to misunderstand
fregare to pinch; to rub
frenare to brake
frequentare to go to; to see
friggere to fry
fuggire to escape
fumare to smoke
funzionare to work
galleggiare to float
garantire to guarantee
gelare to freeze
gestire to manage
gettare to throw
giocare to play
girare to turn
giudicare to judge
giurare to swear
gocciolare to drip
gonfiare to inflate
gonfiarsi to swell
graffiare to scratch
gridare to shout
guadagnare to earn; to gain
guardare to look at; to watch
guarire to cure; to heal up
guastarsi to break down
guidare to drive; to lead
ignorare to ignore
illudersi to deceive oneself
imbiancare to whitewash; to paint
imbrogliare to cheat
imbucare to post
immaginare to imagine; to think
impallidire to go pale
imparare to learn
impazzire to go mad
impedire: impedire a qn di fare qc to stop sb doing sth

impegnarsi: impegnarsi a fare qc to try hard to do sth
impiccarsi to hang oneself
importare to matter; to import
incartare to wrap
incassare to cash
incazzarsi to get pissed off
incendiare to set fire to
inciampare to trip
incominciare to start
incontrare to meet
incoraggiare to encourage
indagare: indagare su to investigate
indebolirsi to get weak
indicare to show; to point to
indirizzare to address; to send
indossare to wear
indovinare to guess
informare:informarsi su qc to ask about sth
ingannare to deceive
ingannarsi to be mistaken
ingelosire to make jealous
ingessare to put in plaster
inghiottire to swallow
ingrandire to enlarge; to extend
ingrassare to make fat
ingrassarsi to put on weight
iniziare to start
innaffiare to water
innamorarsi to fall in love
inquinare to pollute
insegnare to teach
inserire to insert
intasarsi to be blocked
intendere to mean
interrompere to interrupt
intervistare to interview

intitolare to name
intitolarsi to be called
introdurre to introduce; to insert
invecchiare to get old
investire to run over; to invest
inviare to send
invidiare to envy
invitare to invite
iscriversi to register; to enrol; to join
lamentarsi to complain
lanciare to throw; to launch
lasciare to leave
lasciarsi to split up
laurearsi to graduate
lavare to wash
lavarsi i denti to brush one's teeth
lavorare to work
legare to tie
leggere to read
levare to take off
liberare to set free
liberarsi to get away
licenziare to sack; to make redundant
licenziarsi to give up one's job
litigare to quarrel
lottare to fight
lucidare to polish
maledire to curse
maltrattare to ill-treat
mancare to be missing; to be lacking
mandare to send
mangiare to eat
marcire to go rotten
masticare to chew
mentire to lie
meravigliarsi to be surprised
mescolare to mix
mettere to put

migliorare to improve
minacciare to threaten
misurare to measure
molestare to torment; to sexually harass
montare to assemble; to whip up
mordere to bite
morire to die
morsicare to bite
mostrare to show
muovere to move
nascere to be born
nascondere to hide
navigare to sail
  navigare in Internet to surf the Internet
negare to deny
nevicare to snow
noleggiare to hire; to hire out
notare to notice
  farsi notare to draw attention to oneself
nuotare to swim
obbedire to obey
obbligare: obbligare qn a fare qc to make sb do sth
occupare to occupy
  occuparsi di qn to look after sb
odiare to hate
offendere to insult
  offendersi to take offence
offrire to offer
ordinare to order
osare to dare
osservare to observe; to notice
ottenere to get
pagare to pay
parcheggiare to park
pareggiare to draw

parlare to speak; to talk
partecipare to take part in
partire to leave
passare to pass; to call by
passeggiare to stroll
peggiorare to get worse
pendere to hang
pensare to think
  pensare a to think about
perdere to lose; to leak
  perdersi to get lost
perdonare to forgive
permettere to allow
pesare to weigh
  pesarsi to weigh oneself
pescare to fish
pettinare to comb
piacere: mi piace I like it
piangere to cry
piantare to plant; to dump
picchiare to hit; to knock
piegare to fold; to bend
piovere to rain
piovigginare to drizzle
pisciare to piss
pitturare to paint
pizzicare to pinch; to itch
poggiare to place; to put
porre to put; to place
portare to take; to carry; to wear
posare to put
posteggiare to park
potere can
pranzare to have lunch
precipitare to fall
preferire to prefer
pregare to pray
  pregare qn di fare qc to ask sb to do sth

prelevare to withdraw
premere to press
premiare to give a prize to
prendere to take; to get
prenotare to book
preoccupare: preoccuparsi to
  worry
preparare to prepare
prescrivere to prescribe
prestare to lend
  prestare attenzione to pay
  attention
prevedere to foresee; to plan for
procedere to get on
produrre to produce
progettare to plan
proibire to forbid
promettere to promise
proporre to suggest
proteggere to protect
provare to try; to try on; to feel;
  to prove
pubblicare to publish
pulire to clean
pungere to sting
punire to punish
puntare su to bet on
puzzare to stink
raccogliere to collect; to pick
raccomandare to recommend
raccontare to tell
raddrizzare to straighten
radere to shave
  radersi to shave
raffreddare to cool
  raffreddarsi to get cold
raggiungere to reach
ragionare to think
rallentare to slow down

rapinare to rob
rapire to kidnap
rappresentare to represent
rasare to shave off
rassicurare to reassure
reagire to react
realizzare to come true; to realize
recitare to act
recuperare to recover; to get back
regalare to give
reggere to hold
registrare to record
regnare to reign
regolare to adjust
remare to row
rendere to give back
  rendersi conto di qc to realize sth
respirare to breathe
restare to stay; to remain
riaddormentarsi to go back to sleep
ricaricare to reload; to refill; to
  recharge
ricevere to receive
richiamare to call back
richiedere to ask for; to require
riciclare to recycle
ricominciare to start again
riconoscere to recognize
ricordare to remember
  ricordare a qn di fare qc to remind
  sb to do sth
ridare to give... back
ridere to laugh
ridurre to reduce
riempire to fill (in)
rifare to do again
  rifare il letto to make the bed
rifiutare to refuse
riguardare to concern; to consider

rilassarsi to relax
rimandare to put off
rimanere to stay; to remain
rimborsare to refund
rimettere to put back
  rimettersi to recover
rimpiangere to be sorry
rimproverare to tell off
rinchiudere to lock up
rinfrescare to freshen
  rinfrescarsi to freshen up
ringraziare to thank
rinnovare to renew
rintracciare to find
rinunciare to give up
rinviare to postpone
riparare to repair
  ripararsi da to shelter from
ripassare to come back; to revise
riposare to rest
riprendere: riprendersi to recover
riprovare to try again
riscaldare to warm up; to heat
rischiare to risk
risciacquare to rinse
riservare to book
risolvere to solve
risparmiare to save
rispettare to respect
rispondere to answer
ritirare to take out
ritornare to go back; to return
riuscire: riuscire a fare qc to
  succeed in doing sth
rivedere to see again
rompere to break
rotolare to roll
rovinare to ruin
rubare to steal

russare to snore
saldare to settle; to solder
salire to go up; to climb
  salire su to board
  salire in to get into
saltare to jump
salutare to say hello to; to say
  goodbye to
salvare to save; to rescue
sanguinare to bleed
sapere to know; to taste; to smell
sbadigliare to yawn
sbagliare to make a mistake
  sbagliarsi to be wrong
sbattere to slam
sbrigare to do
  sbrigarsi to hurry
sbucciare to peel; to shell
scadere to expire
scaldare to heat
scambiare to exchange
scappare to get away
scaricare to unload; to download
scartare to unwrap; to reject
scavare to dig
scegliere to choose
scendere to go down
  scendere da to get out of; to get
  off
scherzare to joke
schiacciare to squash
sciacquare to rinse
sciare to ski
scintillare to sparkle
sciogliere to dissolve; to undo
scivolare to slip; to slide
scommettere to bet
scomparire to disappear
sconfiggere to defeat

scongelare to defrost
sconsigliare to advise against
scontrarsi to clash; to run into
scopare to sweep
scoppiare to go off; to burst
scoprire to discover
scoraggiarsi to get discouraged
scottare to be hot
  scottarsi to get burnt
scrivere to write
scusare to excuse
  scusarsi to apologize
sdraiarsi to lie down
sedere to be sitting
  sedersi to sit
segnare to mark; to score
seguire to follow
selezionare to select
sembrare to look; to seem
sentire to hear; to feel
  sentirsi bene to feel well
  sentirsi male to feel ill
separare to separate
  separarsi to split up
seppellire to bury
servire to serve
  servire per qc to be for sth
sfidare to challenge
sfogliare to leaf through
sfuggire to escape
sgonfiare to deflate
sgridare: sgridare qn to tell sb off
significare to mean
singhiozzare to sob; to hiccup
sistemare to arrange; to settle
  sistemarsi to settle down; to find a job
slacciare to undo
slegare to untie

smarrire to lose
  smarrirsi to get lost
smettere to stop
smontare to take apart
soddisfare to satisfy
soffiare to blow
sognare to dream
somigliare: somigliare a to look like
sopportare to stand; to put up with
sorpassare to overtake
sorprendere to catch; to surprise
sorridere to smile
sorvegliare to watch
sospettare to suspect
sospirare to sigh
sostenere to support; to claim
sostituire to change
sottolineare to underline
sottovalutare to underestimate
sottrarre to subtract
spaccare to break
sparare to shoot
sparecchiare to clear the table
sparire to disappear
spaventare to scare
  spaventarsi to be scared
spedire to send
spegnere to put out; to turn off
spendere to spend
sperare to hope
spezzare to break
spiegare to explain
  spiegarsi to explain oneself
spingere to push; to drive
spogliare to undress
  spogliarsi to get undressed
spolverare to dust
sporcare to dirty

sposare to marry
  sposarsi to get married
spostare to move
sprecare to waste
spremere to squeeze
sputare to spit
stabilire to fix
  stabilirsi to settle
staccare to remove; to tear out
stampare to print
stancare: stancarsi to get tired
stare to be
  stare fermo to keep still
  stare zitto to be quiet
starnutire to sneeze
stendere to stretch; to hang out
  stendersi to lie down
stirare to iron
stracciare to tear up
strappare to tear up
strillare to scream
stringere to be tight; to clasp
stufarsi: stufarsi di qc to get fed up
  with sth
subire to suffer; to undergo
succedere to happen
sudare to sweat
suicidarsi to commit suicide
suonare to play; to ring
superare to exceed; to overcome;
  to pass
supporre to suppose
svegliare: svegliarsi to wake up
svenire to faint
svestirsi to get undressed
sviluppare to develop
svitare to unscrew
svolgersi to happen
tacere to be quiet

tagliare to cut
tardare to be late
telefonare to phone
  telefonare a qn to phone sb
tenere to hold; to keep
tentare to try
timbrare to stamp
tirare to pull; to throw
toccare to touch
togliere to take off; to take out
tornare to get back; to be back
tossire to cough
tradurre to translate
trascorrere to spend; to pass
trasferire to transfer
  trasferirsi to move
traslocare to move
trasmettere to broadcast
trasportare to carry
trattare to treat
  trattare di to be about
trattenere to hold back
tremare to shake
trovare to find
truccarsi to do one's make-up
tuffarsi to dive
ubriacarsi to get drunk
uccidere to kill
ungere to oil; to grease
unire to put together; to join
  unirsi a to join
urlare to shout
usare to use
uscire to go out
utilizzare to use
valere to be worth
  valere la pena to be worth it
valutare to value
vantarsi to boast

vedere to see
  farsi vedere to be seen
vendere to sell
venire to come
vergognarsi to be ashamed; to be embarrassed
verificare to check
  verificarsi to happen
verniciare to varnish; to paint
versare to pour; to spill; to pay in
vestirsi to get dressed
  vestirsi da to dress up as
viaggiare to travel

vietare to forbid
vincere to win
violentare to rape
visitare to visit
vivere to live
volare to fly
volere to want
  voler bene a qn to like sb; **voler dire** to mean
voltare to turn
votare to vote
vuotare to empty
zoppicare to limp

ENGLISH
INDEX

The words on the following pages cover all of the ESSENTIAL and
IMPORTANT NOUNS in the book.